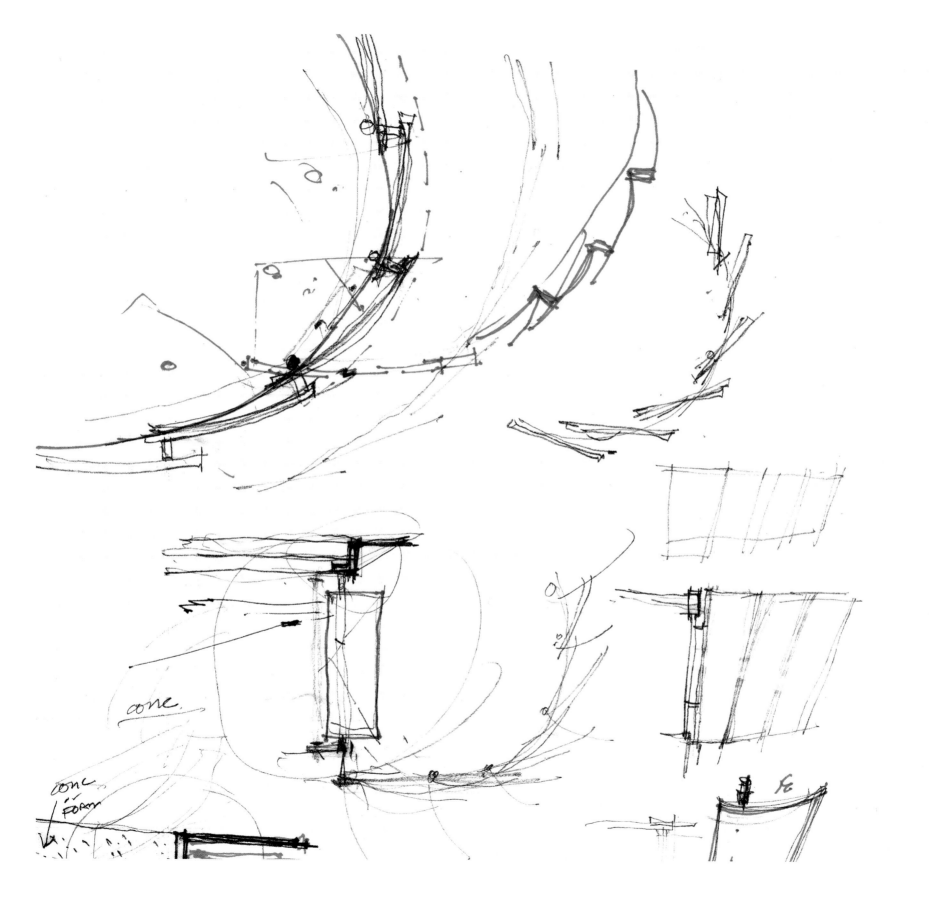

conc.

conc.
form

Caren Yglesias   **Desert Gardens of Steve Martino**
Photographs by Steve Gunther

Foreword by Obie G. Bowman   The Monacelli Press

For Jane

Preface
Caren Yglesias

THERE MAY APPEAR TO BE a conflict between the words 'desert' and 'garden' in the title of this book. "Deserts" bring up associations of dry, infertile, and barren places hostile to people. The word "garden," on the other hand, suggests cultivation, beauty, enclosure, and enjoyment. Why bring these contrasting notions together, except, of course, because that is what Steve Martino has done. Working with desert plants native to the Sonoran Desert, Martino has introduced them to the profession and forever changed cultural conceptions of how gardens can, and should, be part of their region.

This book presents twenty-one desert gardens that span Martino's long career. Included are private gardens that have never been published or are familiar having received numerous awards and extensive publicity. The color photographs were taken by Steve Gunther who patiently waits for the blooming season of the year, and once there, waits for the desired angle of the sunlight and shadow, and even for wildlife to appear. The gardens in person are, if it is possible, even better than these remarkable photographs. I found that they have improved with time. The steel plates rust, bright colors have made their peace with the sun, minerals in the water deposit traces on stucco walls, plants slowly grow. Martino is a master of designing well-scaled outdoor rooms that feel welcoming, comfortable, and encourage lingering even in the desert heat. Often they connect to each other through portals in his looming walls. Moving from garden to garden, new views of startling compositions of plants, walls, and ephemeral shadows lifted from the ground to walls remind me of what all of the world's best gardens can do: transform you through experience. Nowhere is the sun more intense than in the desert or shade more appreciated than under one of Martino's mesquite trees or awning structures. And, in his gardens, the dryness of the desert air is artfully relieved by the sound of water emerging from a single spout and spilling into a small basin. Deserts have oases and Martino's gardens are oases in the city or suburb, as well as the desert.

Martino's designs begin with an inventory of what is within and beyond the site. His obsessive search to provide visual and acoustic privacy and meaningful connections generates constructed frames of desirable views and screen walls that block unwanted sights. Through drawings, Martino studies how to form each element individually and also how they respond to each other in an integrated approach that can only be described as an architectural exploration. No single element stands as an isolated object in a space "filled up" with "features": hearths extend as benches; walls retain earth and water and make distinct boundaries; floor surfaces of various materials abut each other; a few steps define edges; corners nest plants like sculptures. The design is incomplete unless the problems of shade, privacy, and purpose are resolved, and no solution is acceptable if it does not invite living in the garden. I have watched him when he returns to one of his gardens and it's as if he's visiting his plants and wall colors who are old friends that remind him of home. These are the elements of his work that are part of every garden.

As dramatic as these gardens are, their beauty is more than an appearance. Rainwater is a fundamental concern for all desert plant and wildlife. The first inches of rain move across the surface rather than soaking in because, like a dry sponge, the desert floor cannot at first absorb moisture. Sonoran Desert surfaces are particularly hard because of the caliche, a cementious sedimentary rock that binds soil into a salty, impervious layer. Desert plants have adapted by developing shallow, broad root systems to quickly absorb infrequent rainfalls, or by growing extremely deep roots that tap into the more stable aquifer. Networks of washes and waterways called acequia, supply plant communities with collected seasonal rainwater, which support habitats for wildlife in a dynamic balance with the desert climate. Martino's designs protect and restore washes, include plants to restart the ecology of disturbed habitats, and locate places in gardens where people can observe and enjoy the fleeting activity.

As an architect myself it's been interesting to understand Martino's resistance to current construction practices. No bench or fireplace or water basin that comes in a box for installation could possibly be better than custom-making elements that fit exactly in that particular place. More than once I heard him say, "I know a guy with a shop," and together they work out his ideas in fiberglass, metal, glass, and concrete. In other cases, Martino appropriates industrial materials, for example, window flashing woven between steel rebars to make fences and corrugated floor decking on steel frames for sun shades; but they are designed with such imagination that they seem to have found their preferred purpose. This is contrary to standard practices of constructing by assembly, rather than true design and building that driven by the particulars of the site. Perhaps that's why these garden seem timeless and fit so well with the ageless desert. The man-made elements respect their place and command respect by their presence.

When we began this book, Martino suggested I read books by Joseph Wood Krutch, a naturalist who moved to the American Southwest and wrote about the desert in the 1950s. In them, I read about how desert animals and plants survive having adapted to regional conditions centuries ago. Once understood, the interdependent relationships reveal that the austere desert is robust and full of life. There are many lessons for places where water is scarce and cannot be wasted, but not only those places. Martino's desert gardens provide physical demonstrations of how to design and live in recognition of place, with all its constraints and opportunities, and in harmony with an active and healthy ecology. The qualities of the desert become more apparent when seen through these gardens.

Foreword

Obie G. Bowman

STEVE MARTINO'S WORK IS STRIKINGLY THOUGHTFUL with little need of explanation. It is skillful without reliance on, or reference to, the latest imagery of the status quo. It is self-aware, but appropriately so—the result of careful, often intuitive consideration, free of inane archispeak, pettiness, and self-indulgence—wholesome responses to the present and contiguous to both past and future. If they weren't so well orchestrated one might imagine his landscapes having evolved naturally. And perhaps this is the essence of Steve and his work—direct, unaffected, and in keeping with natural forces.

I met Steve in a sculpture class at ASU in the late 1960s, and a bond soon formed between us which has endured to this day. I suspect the spark that ties us together is not unlike the spark that ties so many of us to the greater landscape. It is this special inherent sensibility that enables Steve's greater vision to see through and beyond the obvious.

Steve's interaction with the desert dates back to his troubled delinquent youth and life at the Arizona Boys Ranch where one of his duties was horse wrangling. Lone rides into the desert made unique impressions that helped direct his course and life's work. Years later, after dropping out of architecture school, he began to question why Mediterranean landscapes were so ubiquitous when the existing desert plants seemed more interesting and didn't require life support of water, fertilizers and insecticides. This led to an early career of pioneering work with largely unsympathetic clients and almost no source for the native plants he sought. Backpacking trips around Northern Mexico to gather seeds in the wilderness was his solution and this "can do" attitude continues as the barometer of his life and work. No cheap talk, no excuses, just doing what needs to be done.

This monograph documents the work of a truly engaged and committed designer. Steve Martino is a landscape architect's landscape architect. His work has a depth that is rare to find in this day and age. It not only solves his clients' immediate requirements, but does so with an awareness of the greater context—the landscape as far as the eye can see—the landscape in tune with the way the earth turns—the landscape as compassionate with fellow life forms inhabiting the region. This book not only documents a portfolio of wonderful work, it allows us a glimpse of how we might see ourselves as a species among species in gardens where man and nature can meet with compassion, if not as equals.

The work presented here is the heartfelt, intuitive effort of a man in sync with his time and place. The result is an uncommonly high level of landscape architecture and art. Louis Sullivan defined art as "doing things right" and above all else this book is a testament to "doing things right."

I CALL MYSELF AN ACCIDENTAL LANDSCAPE ARCHITECT. Never having any thoughts in that direction, events put me in the right place at the right time. I was born in Phoenix, Arizona, in 1946. It was an unremarkable city, but it was surrounded by the Sonoran Desert. I left home at thirteen to live on a ranch for my high school years. One of my duties there was that of a wrangler. I frequently spent time horseback riding in the nearby San Tan Mountains where I experienced the desert close up. Growing up in the city, my few previous outings into the desert were during Boy Scout camping weekends.

After high school, I joined the Marine Corps Reserves. After my active duty, I enrolled in Glendale Community College as an art major. One of my instructors suggested I visit Paolo Soleri's studio and workshop in Scottsdale.

I visited the Soleri studio on a Saturday and was struck by what a different world this was compared to anything I had experienced. The place was buzzing with activity: the silt-pile workshops were building structures and the foundry was casting bells. There were architects from Japan, Norway, and England there that day, and of course, the Italian opera was playing.

The next week I sent off my application to the architecture collage at Arizona State University.

One instructor at ASU that had a lasting impact on me was Jerome Deithelm. He taught us how to be observant with his "Leonardo paper" assignments, where we would go out, study something that interested us, and enter our findings in a journal. I think Jerry planted the seeds of landscape architecture.

I enjoyed looking at international design magazines in the architectural college's library. It seemed the grass was greener on the other side of the border. It appeared third world countries had more exciting design than anything I experienced where I lived. As a result, I always looked beyond my environment to the best design I could find for inspiration.

In school, I became interested in the space between buildings to expand the interior space.

My first epiphany came in 1968 when I took a short-lived part-time job as a draftsman for a design-build firm. I had two takeaways. The first was that someone could spend an enormous amount of money on their project, and when they were finished they could still have all the problems they started

with because landscaping was mostly eyewash. The second thing was that landscaping appeared to be a wide-open field. I thought that there must be a huge gap between companies like that and landscape architects, where someone could fit in and make themselves a job. I started doing small landscape projects for relatives and landlords.

I started to develop an interest in site development. I thought it made sense to work for a landscape architect to develop some landscape design skills. I thought all architects should also be landscape architects and do their own site work. It was such an important part of a project that I couldn't imagine turning it over to someone else. Luckily architects don't think that way or we wouldn't have any work.

In 1970, after my third year of architectural school, I had a dirt bike accident. It sidelined my architectural schooling and pushed me into getting a real job. On a good note, I met my wife sixteen years later in the ER after my sixth follow-up surgery.

In 1971 I went to work for Thomas Zimmerman for two years. It was there that I learned the skills of site development. We were working on a townhouse project in Phoenix that was next to a remnant desert lot. We were using all the conventional Mediterranean plants for our project. Looking at the plants that were growing naturally on the adjacent property, I asked, "Why aren't we using those plants, they are growing just on the rain fall while our plants are going to need constant watering and supervision to keep them alive." The answer was, "Those are just weeds." This answer was good enough for the profession, the landscape industry, and the public, but for some reason, not for me. This was probably a "Deithelm" moment. I think not being educated as a landscape architect allowed me to think like that. I decided that I wasn't going to learn more here so I headed off to work in an architectural office where they put me to work doing their site design.

My quest to learn about native desert plants was just starting. There were no books aimed at the landscape usage of native plants. My sources were mostly government publications on topics like "Distribution of Woody Stem Plants" or "Grassland Plants of Arizona." Things changed when I met Ron Gass, who had a small nursery of native plants. He was a walking encyclopedia of knowledge. Several of his plants did not have common names. Since I would not remember Latin names, I hounded him unrelentingly, asking the name of the same plants over and over. Ron was always happy to talk about his plants. In the mid-1970s, a recession put me out of work with the architectural firm and I took this opportunity to go to work in Ron's nursery as a laborer so I could pester him all day long.

I had a few landscape jobs of my own, so this was the start of my career. I made some business cards with the business name "Outdoor Space" on them and decided to market myself to architects. The first four architects that I interviewed with all said, "What the hell is outdoor space?" This was discouraging as the kick-off to my career.

I was starting to take a critical look at Phoenix's man-made character. It wasn't anything special and certainly lacked a sense of a regional identity. It could have been anywhere; fortunately, it was surrounded by the Sonoran Desert. Phoenix was a giant oasis without any special oasis character. It was a place where hundreds of millions of dollars were spent to make it look like someplace else.

The desert was far more interesting to me than anything man-made in the city. Unfortunately, the desert historically was viewed as wasteland where anything done to it was an improvement. The west was a resource to be exploited, and native plants were to be eradicated as worthless vermin.

It never occurred to me to become a landscape architect; I just wanted to use desert plants in my projects, which became the idea to bring the desert into the city. This idea was met with resistance at every step of the way probably because so much effort was being spent on removing the desert.

After the exposed rocks, the most interesting part of the desert are the "dry washes" that come to life after a seasonal rain. It's where the trees are the biggest and the understory plants the most plentiful. Observing how the microclimate created under the trees extends the effectiveness of the spring rains inspired me to mimic this in my gardens. The "wash" became my model for using desert plants.

It seemed that I had to develop the landscape vernacular that should have been here but wasn't. The landscape profession was asleep-at-the-wheel with regards to native plants. Architect John Douglas was quoted in saying that "I had to build my stage before I could act on it."

There was a landscape "style" known as "desert landscaping"; it was pretty much despised by everyone. It was basically gravel, sometimes painted green, with a few cacti or rusty wagon wheels proudly placed around the property. I called these "gardens of despair." They were symbolic notions of a maintenance-free landscape and a prejudiced view of desert planting that absolved the owners of any environmental responsibility.

I, of course, called my work "desert landscaping" as a political statement as much as anything else. I wanted my projects to say something about where we live by celebrating the desert rather than make apologies for it.

When I decided to push native plants, I was pretty much out in left field by myself. I learned from observation and trial and error.

All my projects needed to be demonstration projects for my future clients, the profession, and the public. I remember sitting in my Scottsdale office and seeing a landscape architect in the courtyard pointing out my plants to his client. My pursuit of a "desert landscape style" sidetracked my architectural career.

My success with native plants wouldn't have been possible without the help and encouragement of Ron Gass. In the early days, we would go on seed collecting trips to southern Arizona and northern Mexico. He would grow plants from seeds I brought him. I would try the plants out in different exposures on my projects. I would take my early planting plans to him for his opinion on a horticultural critique rather than a design critique.

I started out to simply create projects that "fit the desert." The obvious way to do that was to use desert plants that could seamlessly connect a project to the adjacent desert.

As my desert gardens started to grow, I noticed that native plants bring along their entourage of pollinators that would activate the garden. Many of these plants had symbiotic pollinators that I had never seen before. It turns out there was another reality right under my nose, and the native plants were the window into that world.

One of my favorite plant stories is watching a strange volunteer sprout in my salvia bed. I let it grow to see what it was. Once it started to branch, I recognized it as 'Scared Datura'. I lived in the city and thought, "Where did this come from?" I couldn't imagine any being within fifteen miles of my house.

It's a night-blooming plant so I went out in the evening to see if the saucer- sized flower had a scent. As leaned over, I was startled by a creature as wide as my hand flying off the flower. I thought it was a bat but it was a Moth Hawk, which had a symbiotic relationship with the plant. My second question was how in the world did the moth find this plant, in my garden, in the city.

I had inadvertently tapped into the food chain, and the gardens were becoming habitats. When I understood this, I think my gardens became interesting.

It became evident that native plants connect the site to its history-timeline, and they represent the most current state of the evolution of a place. It seemed that you could not be more sustainable or practical than using the plants native to the region.

Later, after reading papers by landscape architect Kerry Dawson on the relationship of native plants to the ecosystem, I became more convinced that native plants were the right design choice.

From my observations, it seemed that the landscape profession was so integral to the displacement and destruction of habit that it was more nature-hating than nurturing. I often worked with architects who were more concerned about a site's natural characteristics than landscape architects were.

In the late 1970s, I decided it was time to take the architects exam. When I applied, the state told me that I needed two more years of experience working for architects before I was eligible to even take the exam, but I only needed one more year of experience for the landscape architect's exam. I never had the idea of becoming a landscape architect, but I took the shorter route.

Since I had not gone to landscape school or even had a single landscape class, this seemed daunting. I asked around and found out which books to study. The landscape history books interested me while the civil engineering books put me to sleep. I took the national exam just to see what was on it so I could focus my studying for the next year's exams. To my surprise, I passed all the parts on the first try.

I've described my work as "weeds and walls" which is the juxtaposition of wild landscapes against my refined structures. I thought of the "garden" as a man-made place that would represent nature at its best and man at his best. My approach was to push the garden in a direction and let it evolve over time on its own while in contrast my structures would start to age. I thought that a garden should have a respect for nature rather than be a place to dominate it. Formal parterre gardens and topiary just make me scratch my head; they seem like such wasted energy.

I want the garden to self-propagate and grow beyond its budget. I think not having a landscape education worked to my benefit because I wasn't trained to think like a landscape architect.

When my projects were first entered in the local awards program, the jurors said they couldn't evaluate them against the typical lawn and pine tree landscapes of the time. Their solution was to create a new category called "arid projects," which didn't make me happy. I wanted my projects evaluated against everybody else's. Thirty-five years later, every entered project celebrates the desert while the lawn and pine tree projects are gone.

The first half of my career was a struggle to get clients to use desert plants, which were viewed as weeds. What really got me going was three clients who moved to Phoenix from other parts of the country. They had the resources to build new houses, and they wanted a desert experience, whereas local clients seemed to want to just change the desert.

Once I started to receive national ASLA design awards it seemed to legitimize my work and give me national exposure as magazines started to feature my work.

I started out as a photographer in high school so composition and shadows were always important to me. Here in the desert, it was obvious that the unrelenting sun needs to be seriously considered in design work. I consider it as another building material that can give form to a space.

In school, we were taught that design is a problem-solving exercise, and as a result, my design work was very solution driven and site specific. I found it difficult to do something arbitrary on a project.

A turning point for my career came in 1983 when Cliff Douglas asked me to design an entry for his tree farm, Arid Zone Trees. It was a flat 450-acre site with no problems to solve. It turned out to be a nightmare for me. The more problems a site has, the easier it is to start.

I finally decided that since it was arbitrary, I could do whatever I wanted. I would make it my homage to Luis Barragán, since I loved his work. I borrowed parts from his projects in the 1940s for the design elements. The project was wildly successful, garnering me two national ASLA awards. The project appeared in books and shelter magazines, both here and internationally. After this project started to get published, people began to call me to ask for Barragán-looking colored walls. A benefit of the project was that it was a demonstration project not only for the design profession but also the city administrators, who would come out to look at the garden.

I seem to turn most city gardens into enclosed "courtyard" gardens by creating structures that put edges around the space. I'm a fanatic about creating privacy. Not only do I not want to see the neighbors, I don't want to see their houses and I don't want them seeing me.

Like all designers, I want to make outdoor spaces that people want to be in; I try to do it in a simple straightforward fashion. I want the garden to say something about the site and the region.

In 1986, after my sixth operation, I developed a staph infection from some old hardware in my leg. As a good ending to the long ordeal, I married the nurse who gave me an IV in the emergency room. Jane and I were married in 1988 and a few years later our boys, Hawke and AZ Wolf, came along.

In 1988 Jane and I made a pilgrimage to the Alhambra. As we wandered around the fabulous gardens, the thought struck me that none of the plants could be 900 years old. I was most impressed with the ingenuity of the water systems. A few years later I was thinking about the Court of the Lions, and I couldn't remember if it had any plants in it. I had to pull out my slides, and it did have plants, but they were insignificant. Since plants come and go in the garden, it seemed that plants were incidental to the garden, and it's the architectural space that makes the garden. I thought that gardens need to stand on their own as a space without plants.

I have forty years of experience designing gardens. Clients now come to me with high expectations of what I can do for them. The discussion of sustainability and appropriateness of native plants doesn't even need to come up. This is 180 degrees from where I started.

I was recently in the Palo Cristi garden that I designed twenty years ago. Every time I enter this garden, the cooling shade of the mesquite tree and the visual effect of the water trough makes me say, "It doesn't get any better than this."

Gardens

The sculptural shapes of desert plants appear more striking when strong, plain forms provide the setting.

Opposite: The long, curved driveway follows the slope, which rises more than twelve feet to the house.

Tucson, Arizona

WHEN SUSAN DANIELS AND EUGENE FALK BOUGHT six acres of land in Tucson in 1997, their goal was to maximize the views from this spectacular site to the adjacent Coronado National Forest and downtown Tucson. This area of the undisturbed Sonoran Desert had many restrictions governing construction and desert plant preservation. It also had extremely steep topography that presented challenges for any design. The clients hired New York architect Bart Voorsanger to design a new house to take advantage of the extraordinary views. They asked Martino to develop the outdoor spaces and solve the grading problems. With the proximity of the forest and desert, he was determined to make the project fit the site by seamlessly connecting it them and views of the distant mountains.

Throughout the three-year construction process, great care was taken to avoid disturbing the site beyond the house footprint. The preliminary construction of the pool and terraces allowed those areas to be used to stage the rest of the house construction.

Martino prefers to avoid standard engineering mitigating remedies to grading difficulties. Instead of a perimeter drainage channel proposed by the engineers, Martino located a drop inlet behind a retaining wall to direct the surface run-off through a culvert buried below the new terraces that empties back into the wash on the east side of the house where the rainwater can continue to flow. Then he designed the multiple terraces and retaining walls to step up and down in response to the natural terrain, much like the way the house roofs are canted to capture and frame mountain peak views.

The designed gardens and terraces occupy nearly three-quarters of an acre. One of Martino's design goals was to provide a direct and enticing path out of every door into the desert. At the front of the house, a runnel connects a water trough on the lower level with the entry fountain, drawing attention away from the driveway and garage doors, and keeping the focus on the entry and gardens. A runnel in the Royal Alcázar Palace courtyard in Seville, Spain, inspired the design of another runnel in the retaining wall outside the master

bedroom garden. The recirculating water spills into a water trough that has become a local watering hole for wildlife.

Martino sited the infinity-edge pool and adjacent retaining walls to extend out from the house into the desert and lead the eye toward the mountains. The rear property line is about forty feet beyond the pool edge, but the absence of a man-made fence allows the garden to flow into the adjacent landscape. Tucson has a pool safety fence option that allows existing vegetation barriers and planted cactus to be used in lieu of a traditional pool fence. Similarly, native desert plants blur the precise location of the property edge.

Martino's site walls and grading design give the impression that this house is nestled into the land rather than perched on it. This close fit helps the house and garden belong to and even celebrate their place in the desert.

Desert gardens were planted under and around the open-tread stairs to direct attention away from the parking area.

POOL

BED BED OFFICE PATIO PATIO

BATH BED LIVING FAMILY ROOM

PATIO

LOWER PATIO

COURTYARD

GARAGE LOWER LEVEL

DRIVE

GUEST PARKING

DRIVE

0   15'   30'   50'

Opposite: The master bedroom
has a deep roof overhang that
blocks the intense summer sun
and frames mountain views.

Below: The gardens include a runnel that drops water
into the wildlife watering hole below.

Retaining walls and terraces
surrounding the pool follow
the original contours.

31

Desert boulders appear to extend into the pool in a harmony of extremes. The negative edge pool makes the water look like it's falling into the hillside. The reflections in the water reinforce the connections between constructed elements and the land.

Opposite: The orientation of the lap lane visually links the house and desert.

Left: This garden is a blend of antique artifacts and contemporary art carefully placed in courtyards full of native desert plants.

Opposite: Six-foot-high masonry walls and eight-foot-high steel plates provide privacy from the street. They are set back to leave room for gardens along the sidewalk.

City Grocery Garden

Phoenix, Arizona

GEORGIA BATES IS AN INTERIOR DESIGNER who loves remodeling work. In 2006 she found a rundown grocery store on an 8,700-square-foot corner lot in the heart of Phoenix and bought it along with the adjacent aging bungalow. These old markets, which once served residential neighborhoods, are now sought after by artists and designers for their loft-like spaces. Georgia saw an opportunity to create a work-live compound with garden courtyards.

Martino was asked to help with the site improvements and landscape design. The concept was to turn the former delivery area behind the store into a common courtyard shared by the residence and studio. The two buildings were gutted, and sliding-glass doors were inserted into the walls where the structures face each other. The building uses were reversed with the bungalow becoming Bates's studio and the store her residence.

The studio floor was two-and-a-half feet higher than that of the residence. To connect the two buildings, Martino added a new landing and stairs that are the same width as the central courtyard. A raised planter was built at one side of the stairs and around an original masonry wall, which brought the garden up to the studio floor level. A simple corrugated steel roof covers the courtyard, a material commonly used in neighborhoods such as this one, which were built from the late 1920s up until World War II.

Masonry and steel-sheet walls surround the property, completely blocking views of the adjacent intersection. On the west side, Martino designed a new pedestrian entry where a service drive had been. On the north side, a freestanding fireplace is part of the wall that ends of the long view from the studio, through the courtyard and residence interior, to the north patio. A new fountain wall, which also hides a storage area and pump, was built in the courtyard on the eastern side of the property. This is a typical Martino fountain with a small discharge pipe that protrudes through a metal panel, which gives the spout more visual impact. On the west side of the studio, the patio level is raised to create a balcony-like space that overlooks the street.

Three utility poles and five tall palm trees were already on the site. Martino incorporated the palm trees into the new planting scheme and added plants that are frequently used in the area, including Prickly Pear cactus (*Opuntia*), Creosote bush (*Larrea tridentata*), and Texas Sage (*Leucophyllum frutescens*). New canopy trees — native Palo Verde (*Parkinsonia x Desert Museum*) and Mesquite (*Prosopis velutina*) — were planted to shade the courtyard and garden. The desert plants in all the gardens bring a bit of the Sonoran Desert back into the urban environment.

The entry off the sidewalk introduces the garden materials: native desert plants, crushed stone ground cover, unadorned walls, and rusted steel elements.

Below: Wide concrete stairs and a deep landing extend the studio space into the courtyard.

Opposite: The new planter wraps around an existing masonry wall. The covered porch on the studio's west side was raised to floor level to make a shady place that overlooks the street.

An opening cut into an existing masonry wall directly opposite the new steel entry gate allows a layered view of several small gardens.

DRIVEWAY

SLEEP

COURTYARD

PATIO

LIVING

DINING

PATIO

STUDIO

KITCHEN

0   20'

Left: The constructed vocabulary of industrial materials includes exposed cinder block piers that support steel pipe columns and a corrugated steel roof.

Opposite: The fountain wall defines the back edge of the central courtyard and conceals storage space behind.

Captured space between the former store and new wall at the sidewalk creates room for a private garden around a fireplace.

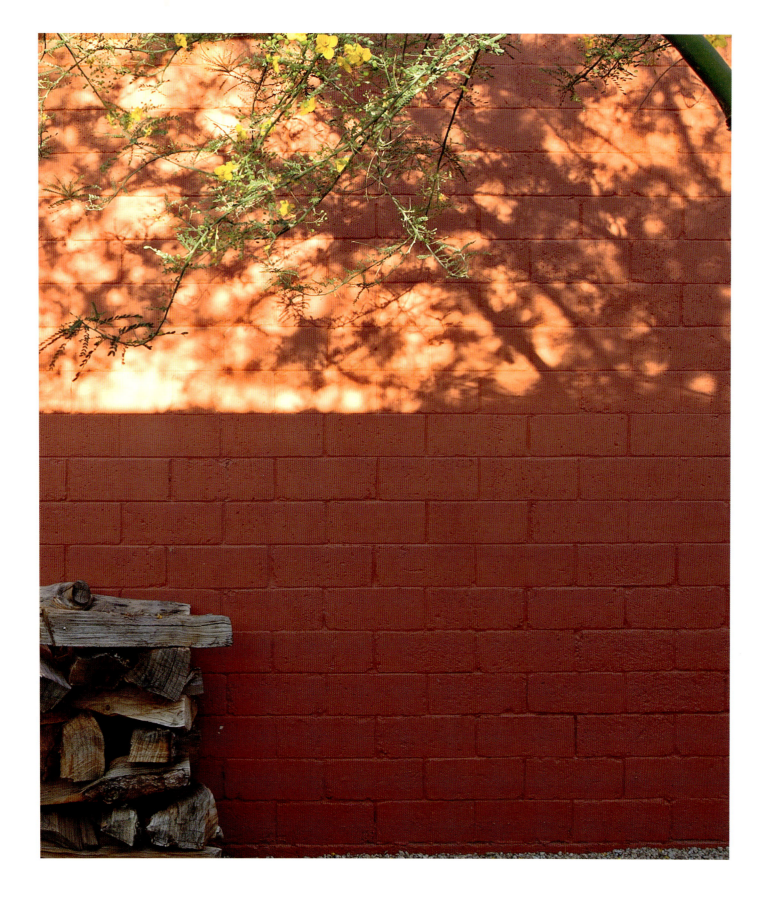

The path in a side garden provides a place to store firewood and the client's collection of antique terra-cotta honey pots.

Like Martino's translucent walls, the surface of the water makes a plane that reflects the plants and garden elements. The clients' beloved 100-year-old garden sculpture, installed above the pool fountain, adds a figural element to the scene.

Paradise Valley, Arizona

TERRY GREENE AND WALT STERLING HAD an unusual backyard. It was shallow but very wide — 50 by 210 feet — with views of the neighboring houses over a six-foot high wall. Adding a pool and screening views of the adjacent properties were the major goals of the project.

The back of the house had a long covered patio that ran its full length. Martino decided to design the pool as a third rectangle and placed it parallel to the porch and house, setting up a sequence from the enclosed interior rooms to the surface of open water with a covered outdoor room in between.

Working with a very tight budget, Martino took advantage of a fortieth-anniversary sale offered by a local pool contractor. He then reduced the pool's buried depth by eighteen inches to save excavation costs. The excavated soil was used to build up the raised deck and make landscape berms to break up the flat site. The pool excavator who spread the dirt even dug a depression to exaggerate the site's new terrain.

The concrete pool shell is left partially exposed above the ground on three sides, and the side closest to the house has a concrete cap that allows it to double as a long bench. The back two pool walls have a chamfered top that gives a "near-negative" edge look and reduces the appearance of bulky concrete edges. If water splashes out of the pool, it just drops down to the ground.

The plants and trees were mostly the smallest available size when planted. There was so much space to fill that Martino instructed the clients to trim just a few trees next to the house and let the others grow to the ground, which is their natural form. Desert trees only have exposed trunks when they are manicured for landscape use or cattle have eaten away the lower branches. By letting the trees grow to the ground, they take up more space and understory plants are not needed. This was a landscape experiment that proved to be a workable idea.

A low wall around the front yard made a courtyard, but did not effectively enclose the space and block views to the street and houses beyond. Martino designed two tall freestanding masonry walls to screen views from the house with a recessed outdoor fireplace in one and a spout for water to fall into a small pool in the other. The walls not only create privacy, but also create a sense of perspective and depth when viewed from the interior spaces. Again, this space was planted with the smallest of trees, knowing that they will grow. As Martino says, "A terrific garden just takes time and water, and everybody knows that the smaller the installed plant, the better it will grow." Patience was a required element in this landscape design. Now, six years later, the garden has found its full form.

In the front yard, two red walls define areas and block unwanted views. The wall closer to the house contains a recessed outdoor fireplace and the other wall a water fountain and low basin.

Opposite: The upper fireplace terrace is nearly level with the pool surface, which expands the sense of space.

Left: The long side of the pool provides extra seating.

The crisp edge of the pool contrasts with the soft shapes of the plants, many of which started as cuttings from Martino's garden.

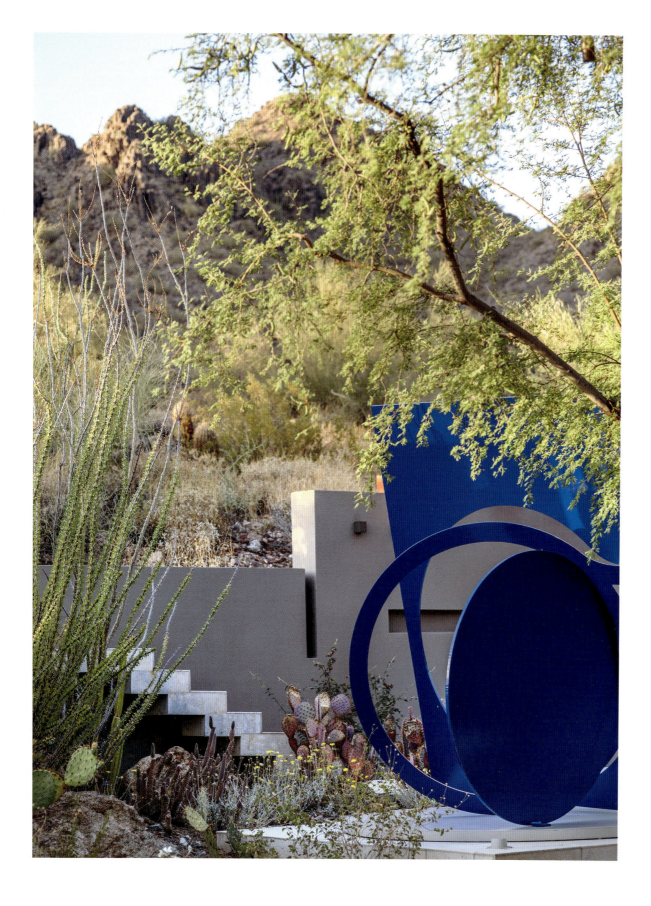

Left: The cantilevered concrete stairs connect the terrace to the desert beyond the property line.

Opposite: A large Saguaro cactus (*Carnegiea gigantea*) was brought in as a focal point. Its vertical form contrasts with the cantilevered horizontal beams that are part of the shade structure.

Phoenix, Arizona

STRONG ARCHITECTURAL LINES and unornamented surfaces are the foundation of this garden design. Martino's intention was to use a palette of walls, plants, water, sunlight, and sculpture to establish and accentuate relationships between garden and house, and between garden and desert.

The nearly one-acre site is adjacent to the Phoenix Mountains Preserve, a large park of small mountains and foothills that interrupt the flat land and city grid. A small knoll effectively hides views of neighboring houses, and the desert appears to extend from the terrace to the mountain peaks beyond. This situation was the perfect opportunity for Martino to use the landscape concept of "borrowed scenery."

The clients, Denise and Robert Delgado, had lived in the house for almost twenty years before Martino began this project. The existing garden had large boulder retaining walls that were an expedient solution to handle the steep hillside, but the result was incongruous with the clean architectural lines of the house and took up too much space. Gradually, the clients' interest in contemporary art prompted them to reconceive the garden as an outdoor gallery. In redesigning, Martino was asked to showcase two large contemporary sculptures.

The scheme lowered the upper terrace level by three feet and expanded the garden to the west along existing contours to minimize the need for further hillside grading. New and existing masonry retaining walls extending across the site provide a unifying architectural backdrop for the spaces and sculptures. Planes of smooth stucco walls shift back and forth to make small gaps that introduce depth and a sense of mystery through the play of light and shadow. Along the sides, frosted glass panels step up the hillside, providing privacy and capturing the movement of nearby plants caught in the wind.

A ceramic sculpture by Japanese artist Jun Kaneko terminates the axis from the entry doors, through the living room, over a small pool of water and fountain spout, to the terrace. A painted-steel sculpture by American artist Fletcher Benton anchors the perpendicular east-west axis. Intense late afternoon sunlight pours through the sculpture's openings, casting constantly changing shadows. The placement of the two sculptures make them an integral part, and not just an added ornament, of the garden design.

The clients remodeled their house in response to the new garden. Full-height folding glass doors replaced smaller windows and framed doors. When open, the glass walls allow the interior rooms and the garden to flow seamlessly together. Martino set the new water pool edge only one foot away from the living room, and this close proximity blurs the boundary between house and garden as the surface reflections and fountain sounds are part of both spaces.

The translucent glass panels are dappled with shadows as plants move with the wind during the day. They are backlit to provide a similar effect at night.

Below: The rear retaining wall supports a "floating" limestone bench that extends into the fireplace and becomes its hearth.

Below: The Fletcher Benton sculpture sits on a rotatable base that can be turned to vary the cast shadows and views through the openings.

Right: Stainless steel spider-fittings support overlapping translucent glass panels that step up the hill.

A shade structure composed of eight cantilevered steel beams projects from the wall. A protective canvas tonneau cover snaps in place when more shade is desired. When the cover is off, the beams create a dynamic sundial effect of linear shadows that move across the garden floor and wall throughout the day.

VEGETABLE GARDEN

SCULPTURE

PROPERTY LINE

TERRACE

SCULPTURE

SPA

GARDEN

BEDROOMS

DESERT

GLASS FENCE

LIVING

BEDROOMS

GARAGE

WASH

0   40'

The surface of the water is nearly level with the bedroom terrace. The sides of the pool were designed so that the water falls over edges to the lower terrace and living room level thereby connecting the spaces visually and acoustically. The Jun Kaneko ceramic sculpture terminates the view from the interior.

The west garden displays the contrast between refined materials and rugged desert plants.

The sheds and fiberglass panel completely block views of the street and sidewalk beyond, creating a private courtyard. The site was the proverbial tabula rasa and completely devoid of plants.

Phoenix, Arizona

CAROLYN HARTLEY WAS THRILLED TO FIND this house in a quiet Phoenix neighborhood. The location shortened her commute to work significantly, and the property was across from the South Mountain Park/Preserve, which at more than 16,000 acres and encompassing three mountain ranges, is one of the largest urban parks in the world. But she did not anticipate the steady stream of hikers walking behind the property on their way to a nearby popular trailhead. An eight-foot high retaining wall separated her backyard from the public sidewalk, but the path was seven feet higher than the backyard. As a result, she had no privacy and did not open the curtains or venture out into the backyard.

In 2011 Martino was commissioned to design the landscape, and he immediately knew that privacy was needed before plants could be considered. He was intrigued by the severity of the site problems and thought that this 9,000-square-foot lot would be a good case study to try out some ideas he had been developing.

The first step was to determine what could be done to block views from the public sidewalk. Trees were ruled out because the maximum screen height had to be controlled if the client was to be able to see the distant mountains. Martino concluded that a thirteen-foot wall was needed, but city regulations do not allow such high walls. Ironically, accessory buildings or sheds can be fifteen feet high. If less than 200 square feet, they can be built without a building permit, and standard setbacks from the property line don't apply. Martino thinks of sheds as a designer's "wild-card" and often incorporates them in projects that lack privacy. Here, he designed two sheds to effectively block all evidence of the busy sidewalk. The two structures were required to be six feet apart, which left a gap in the privacy screening. To remedy that situation, Martino designed a translucent fiberglass sliding door that is mounted on one shed and can be opened to fill the gap and make a continuous wall.

This project used every trick in Martino's book: the fireplace shed has a cantilevered shade structure and the observation shed has a grand stair inspired by the Villa Malaparte in Capri. At the top of the stairs, the client can see the mountains without looking at the sidewalk because the stair landing is higher. In the opposite direction, views of downtown city lights turned out to be an unexpected bonus of the design.

Before Martino's work, this backyard was exposed, noisy, and uninviting. The design transformed it into a large garden room. Tall sheds make a back edge that removes the public from the garden experience while also creating a dominate view when seen from the house. Crushed rock is used as ground cover to make the space feel more open. Close to the house, a small water trough, which was inspired by the quiet pool and fountain in the early sixth century Bagh-e Fin Palace garden in Kashan, Iran, offers cooling relief from the desert heat. Native desert plants provide shade and connect the garden to the greater regional ecology. The newly achieved privacy along with the arrival of butterflies and hummingbirds have brought the client out into the garden on a daily basis. The dramatic red walls supplied the privacy, and the native desert plants created the garden atmosphere and sense of place.

A canopy of steel beams and perforated-steel screen panels projects from the shed to block the intense sun. A ledge breaks up the tall wall, and the hearth wraps the fireplace for additional seating.

The stepped roof of the observation shed is also a stair leading to the observation deck.

The charcoal-colored stucco wall accentuates the cantilevered stair projection and provides a place for the site-cast concrete bench.

The observation deck overlooks the garden and provides
panoramic views of the distant
mountains.

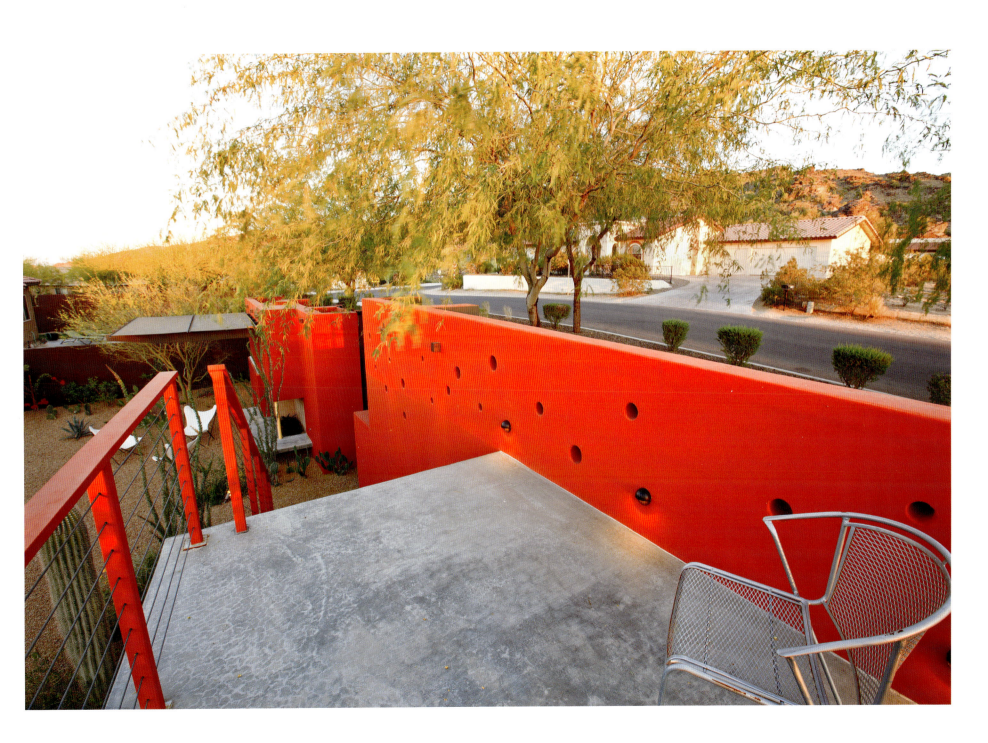

Martino designed a row of hanging fabric panels to shade the dining area.

Opposite: The broad ledge of a raised site-cast concrete planter adds interest to a corner of the garden.

CITY SIDEWALK

FIREPLACE SHED   OBSERVATION SHED

METAL SCREEN
SHADE STRUCTURE   GARDEN ROOM

WATER

PATIO

LIVING ROOM   BEDROOM

KITCHEN

ENTRANCE   GARAGE

BEDROOM

DRIVEWAY

0   20'

A composition of planes, zig-zags, and circles in a deep red and charcoal palette is a dramatic backdrop to the garden room. Stickman cactus (*Nopalea cochenillifera*) come from a specimen given to Martino, who then cultivated a piece to add to his clients' gardens.

The garden looks well established because mature Blue Palo Verde (*Parkinsonia florida*) and Desert Ironwood (*Olneua tesota*) trees were obtained from a salvage company and installed. The cactus are from Martino's garden.

The cerulean blue wall juxtaposed with magenta flowers of bougainvillea and common Prickly Pear or Indian Fig cactus (*Opuntia ficus-indica*) evokes the brilliant palette of Mexican architect Luis Barragán.

Paradise Valley, Arizona

CYNTHIA AND WILLIAM TURNER HAD COMMISSIONED Martino to design a pool and terrace for their previous home. At that time, they told him that in about twenty years they would sell that house and buy a smaller hillside house on the Camelback Inn Resort property and hire him to remodel the house and gardens. And twenty years later, they did indeed call him to say they had bought a house and wanted him to remodel it.

Excited by the opportunity, Martino was disappointed when he saw that the house seemed to be one of the ugliest in the entire development. It was made of slump block, with a big arched entry and few windows to take advantage of the surrounding views. Four-foot roof overhangs projected over the tight exterior spaces. The only way to add additional interior space was to reduce the width of the entry and eliminate one bay of the garage.

The Turners wanted to evoke Luis Barragán's house in Mexico City. Martino realized that would require recladding all the exterior surfaces and altering the roof by cutting off roof overhangs, adding parapets, and replacing load-bearing walls with roof beams to open up the interior space. These changes accommodated new ceiling-height sliding glass doors that opened onto enclosed garden courtyards. Interior walls could be removed to create vistas through the house to the gardens. The sunken living room floor was raised to make it level with the terrace and the roof was raised by four feet.

Also problematic was the original entry walk, which shared the driveway and sloped eighteen inches. Martino redesigned the entry by removing part of the driveway and raising the path to street level. This leads to a long exterior passage that extends past an interior garden courtyard. Now the view from the entry extends over the blue fountain wall to the mountains above.

The west side of the property is adjacent to a tree-lined wash in the desert that was unseen from the garden. Martino replaced the existing wall along the property line with a lower three-step bench, which provided seating and allowed the wash and its vegetation to become part of the garden.

The rear wall, already the maximum height permitted by code, did not conceal the neighboring roof. Martino added steel panels in strategic places to act as blinders and raise that portion of the wall by sixteen inches. One of the panels has a fountain spout in it, bringing water into the garden as it falls into a small pool. Narrow linear terraces at the back and side of the house used every square inch of land.

Cynthia Turner, the artist in the family, chose the colors for the walls. Her husband was skeptical at the beginning of the project, but by the end, he admitted that the purple wall running from the courtyard through the house to the outdoor dining area "couldn't be anything else."

The narrow entrance opens up into a courtyard filled with desert plants in many shapes and textures, including *Dasylirion*, Ocotillo (*Fouquiria splendens*), and common Prickly Pear (*Opuntia ficus-indica*).

An opening in the wall above the pool offers a view of the mountains from the master bedroom.

		WATER	
LAWN	PATIO		WASH
BATH			
		LIVING ROOM	
LIBRARY			
BEDROOM		PATIO	
		KITCHEN	
WATER	COURTYARD		
GARDEN	GUEST	LAUNDRY	GARAGE	STUDY
	STORAGE		STORAGE
	ENTRY		

0   10'   25'

Opposite: A ribbed glass panel protects the privacy of the guest bedroom.

Below: A canopy stretched between the guest quarters and the main house shades the courtyard and the surrounding windows.

The brilliant color of the
entrance courtyard contrasts
with a monochromatic
palette in the rear.

Parts of the perimeter wall were replaced with step seating so that the trees could be seen and the garden could meet the desert.

Palo Cristi Garden

This garden of walls, water, and desert plants connects the house to the adjacent wash.

Paradise Valley, Arizona

THIS LOT WAS THE LAST TO SELL in its subdivision. There were streets on three sides, and the land was bisected diagonally by a wide drainage easement, which protected a naturally occurring wash or arroyo. The lot had been cleared, and some time in the past, it had become an illegal dump site for construction debris.

The clients clearly understood the positive attributes of the site, especially the wash with its mature native trees. Other advantages were the desert on the west side of the property, which was unusual for the area, and expansive mountain views. Looking for inspiration, the clients visited Luis Barragán's house in Mexico City in the mid-1990s and returned with a stack of books on his work, which they handed to Martino. They asked if he could design gardens in a similar style.

Unfortunately, the subdivision did not share their values. In this part of Phoenix, typically, the desert is suppressed and a mini "Tuscan villa," complete with Mediterranean plants, replaces the native habitat. Martino does not agree with this design approach. His goal is to create an experience — a garden as threshold — to transport people away from the city and immerse them in a desert environment. This garden would become part of the desert through its spaces, materials, colors, and plants.

Martino stretched the driveway to the auto court from the far corner of the property to make the entry experience as long and interesting as possible. This drive through the desert starts in a tight, tree-covered space, crosses the wash, and then turns to reveal a distant view of the house down a tree-lined gravel road. It ends at the auto court surrounded by native trees and cactus.

The clients designed the house themselves as a modern interpretation of a historic hacienda with courtyards and wells. To protect the interior from the intense morning and afternoon sun there are few windows in the northeast and southwest walls. The northwest and southeast walls are mostly glass, which opens up the house to views of the wash to the north and exposes the south-facing courtyard to the winter sun. Martino designed two water troughs that attract wildlife, but not all wildlife is welcome. Courtyard walls keep rabbits out of the vegetable garden and provide privacy from the street.

The project has only a few small areas of concrete paving. Martino observed that any construction activity unearthed a very rocky sub-surface that clearly reflected the local character more than the manicured crushed-rock topping typically applied to landscapes as ground cover. He had the site tilled before planting to expose these fist-sized rocks and then used them as the finished ground covering for the entry drive, auto court, walkways, and courtyard to allow the constructed surfaces to blend with the natural desert floor beyond the site.

The regenerative planting design added ninety new trees to the twenty existing trees in the wash. Native shrubs that would reseed themselves were used, and a native plant seed mix was applied to the disturbed areas of the site.

After twenty years, the clients decided to make some changes. The iconic Martino blue wall-fountain trough needed repair. Martino added another wall and changed the water trough design. On the other side of the house, the lawn was no longer needed and the clients thought an outdoor fireplace would be good for cool evening gatherings. The new "Barragán-influenced" fireplace wall and constructed swale that leads to the wash completely removed all vestiges of the old lawn area. Plants were relocated or trimmed to open long views across the property and down the wash.

In this project Martino turned a vacant lot strewn with construction debris and bound with development restrictions into a very special place in the desert in which the house and garden are in harmony with the landscape. The use of native plants created a habitat garden that is directly linked to the wash and region. The garden has a very wild and natural look to it. It provides food and shelter to birds and animals, and something is always in bloom for butterflies and hummingbirds. The project is a seminal demonstration of an appropriate design response in the sensitive and fragile desert environment.

The wall of the Casita is planted with agaves (*Agave americana*) and a Desert Ironwood tree (*Olneya tesota*).

Left: The fountain in the south courtyard can be seen from the living room.

Opposite: A niche in the wall of the entry courtyard.

Opposite: Variegated Agave (*Opuntia engelmannii*), harvested from elsewhere in the garden, are now planted around the blue wall fountain.

Right: View from the covered patio to the rust-colored wall.

ENTRY

WEEDS & WILDFLOWERS

FIRE PLACE

DRIVEWAY

DRAINAGE EASEMENT

PATIO

BED

LIBRARY

CASITA

KITCHEN

GARAGE

DINING

ENTRY

LIVING

DRIVEWAY

COURTYARD

GUEST

AUTO COURT

0   15'   30'   50'

Rocks cover the ground that
connects the terrace to the
wash beyond.

Above: The strong, linear geometry of the house shelters furnishings and plants.

Opposite: Sounds from the
blue wall fountain animate the
south courtyard.

Below: The water trough
directs the view to the desert.

This backyard became a
courtyard garden enclosed
by walls that capture and
display the light and
shadows of the morning sun.

Phoenix, Arizona

MARTINO SAW THIS PROJECT AS AN OPPORTUNITY to demonstrate how a typical suburban backyard could be transformed into a private outdoor garden room. As with many suburban houses, the backyard is next to a public alley, with neighboring houses on either side and across the alley. The clients, Nita and Jan Keiser, wanted to make the space more usable and reduce the amount of energy needed for the oversized pool that dominated the small space.

Martino replaced the free-form pool with a rectangular design that connected to the surrounding hardscape elements in a unified composition. As in many of his projects, Martino utilized one of his favorite "secret weapons": the shed. As "accessory buildings" according to building codes, these structures can be higher and closer to property lines than otherwise allowed. Martino uses them to give private gardens the enclosure they need for privacy.

Here, a shed with an open, corner fireplace, placed directly opposite the main interior rooms, became a focal point of the house and concealed the houses beyond. The hearth extends further than what is strictly needed for the fireplace and becomes a built-in bench. Another shed at the far end of the pool, built of fiberglass panels in a steel frame, is a translucent wall that plays with shadows during the day and becomes a wall of light at night.

Even with a smaller pool, the areas for plants was very limited. Martino planted fruitless olive trees (*Olea europaea*) and yuccas (*Yucca rostrada*) next to the pool and a Blue Palo Verde tree (*Parkinsonia florida*), a semi-evergreen, thornless hybrid, next to the patio edge. In the spirit of another Martino saying, "Kill the lawn and save your grandchildren," the lawn was removed and a garden of native desert plants was added.

The Keisers rarely used the original backyard, but with the new design, completed in 2010, they live outside a great deal of the time. This experience prompted the redesign of the front yard, which was completed six years later. That project created a private entry court for sitting out of view from the street with a walk and small fountain built into the side of a planter. This garden has become the focus of the front interior rooms, obscuring the houses across the street. The lawn and three massive frost-tender Ficus trees were replaced with desert plants and crushed-rock ground cover. To the delight of the Keisers, hummingbirds visit their gardens year round.

Above: A concrete walk leads past a raised planter to an entry garden of desert plants and a small pool.

Right: In the side yard, common Prickly Pear cactus (*Opuntia ficus-indica*) stand out against the red wall.

Opposite: The wall along the alley was painted black to make the yard look deeper and provide a backdrop for a pair of Big Bend yuccas (*Yucca rostrada*) that break up the flat surfaces especially when the morning sun casts shadows on the adjacent wall.

The back-wall panels are staggered to accommodate a fireplace in the corner with a raised concrete hearth for extra seating. The small light fixtures have a stronger presence when installed as pairs.

The backlit translucent wall of the shed animates the view from the house at night.

The curved fountain wall was inserted in the rear corner of the yard, creating an unexpected geometry in the rectilinear space.

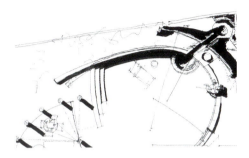

Phoenix, Arizona

THIS SMALL GARDEN is very special to Martino. He says it got him going as a designer. The client, Jay Hawkinson, is an industrial designer who spends his days in a high-rise office building either in Phoenix or Chicago. When he bought this house in 1986, he commissioned Martino to provide a landscape design for the corner lot, which backs up to a desert on public land. Martino came up with a modernist design, which included a swimming pool, outdoor grill, fountain, and fireplace in the side yard, and said it was *Sunset* magazine material. The client built the entry and terrace in the backyard that connects to the desert, and stopped there.

For four years, work on the side yard was deferred while Hawkinson made improvements to the interior of the house. He confessed that he could not imagine taking care of a swimming pool, especially given his travel schedule. When Martino saw the interior, he decided that this client would be receptive to something out of the ordinary.

The side yard plan was redesigned as an outdoor desert room, without a swimming pool or much paving. Privacy was more of an issue the second time around. Since six feet was the maximum wall height permitted, Martino lowered the garden by a foot to make the wall effectively seven feet high and the space to feel more contained. The slight level change was made more dramatic by broad curved steps. A Barragán-inspired fountain was designed for the corner. The water runnel aligns with the sight line from the glass doors of the house back into the fountain alcove. The curved shape repeats in new site walls and a metal gate.

Two Blue Palo Verde trees (*Parkinsonia florida*) that came up from seed during the four-year project hiatus were incorporated along with additional desert trees and plants. Cactus cuttings were added, and today, after twenty years, the small cactus pads have become impressive trees.

The goal of this design was to create a private sanctuary that was a refuge from the time the client spends in high-rise buildings. Now Hawkinson can sit with his lemonade under the canvas awning and count hummingbirds. One lesson Martino learned with this project is that the better the designer knows the client, the easier to match the garden design to his needs. Martino also realized that gardens don't need a lot of bells and whistles. The basic garden requirements are a tree, a wall, a place to sit in the shade, and a little water. To make a bigger garden, simply add more of these elements.

Left: Magenta poles support the yellow canvas awning bringing year-round color into the garden.

Opposite: The shaded patio looks over the garden and fountain structure. Three curved steps adjust the slope into two level terraces.

WEEDS & WILDFLOWERS

WATER

PATIO

PATIO

RESIDENCE

GARAGE

0   20'

Below left:
A blue concrete pyramid terminates the axial view from the house.

Below right and opposite:
Tones and textures with subtle variations make up an articulated display of desert plants. Grown together over time, the cacti form a single living sculpture.

The water channel and
fountain chamber align with
views from the house and
the sound of the water
masks noise from the
adjacent street. The surfaces
of the wall, runnel, and pool
have accrued the patina of
time. At night, dramatic
lighting reveals the layers of
the composition.

Blue Palo Verde trees
(*Parkinsonia florida*), the state
tree of Arizona, are reflected in
the pool. They bloom every
spring when desert plants
come alive with brilliant colors.

Paradise Valley, Arizona

AFTER TRAVELING THROUGH A NEIGHBORHOOD of expensive but unremarkable houses, Martino was delighted when he first saw this project site. Instead of a house in a pseudo-Mediterranean style typical of the area, he found an eccentric addition under construction.

In 1999 the owners, a journalist and an attorney, hired architect John Douglas to expand their home, and they wanted Martino to design gardens to connect the buildings, create a new front entry, and provide shade for an existing swimming pool. The property had desert plants, but the clients hoped the new design would amplify the character of their desert setting and provide privacy from the street and neighbors.

The goal of the project was to link outdoor spaces that were isolated by the odd configuration of the house in an artful way that was clear and direct. On the one hand, the sheer drama of the adjacent mountains would overpower a typical garden, and on the other, any new garden design would have to hold its own against the architecture and the harsh environment. Martino needed to design spaces that were formed by bold materials in an entirely new way.

The first step was to move the existing straight driveway that bisected the land off to one side. This shift turned the front yard into a larger area and when replanted, cut off views from the street to the house. As part of the work, the original contours of the site, which had been altered by the driveway, were restored.

To clarify the hidden entrance and direct movement between gardens, Martino composed a new arrangement of elements, including low walls, paths with tapered shapes, and a fountain to help orient people toward different parts of the house and office.

Martino remodeled the original pool, enlarged the surrounding deck, and added a new concrete-and-steel pavilion to shade the grill area that looks out over the pool to a spectacular view of the mountains. The required safety fence was set off at a distance to make the pool seem as if it was in the open desert. Next to the pool is a tilted outdoor shower wall that stands out like a garden folly. The cliffs of Camelback Mountain inspired this wall, an element that is repeated throughout the gardens to provide a sense of unity and to define specific garden areas in the nearly one-and-one-half acre landscape. Strategically placed, slot-like portals between these walls encourage movement from one garden to another.

The pool area is connected to other gardens by a path called Canyon Walk because of its narrow width and sense of tension created by its high angled walls. It leads to a new dining terrace with a concrete fountain that matches the new entry fountain design.

A special garden showcases plants and rock from the Baja region of the Sonoran Desert that the clients liked to visit. Occupying a back corner of the site, this area was unused because the adjacent wash was littered with construction debris and overgrown with a row of non-native Tamarisk trees. Martino designed the Baja Garden as a sunken amphitheater-like room with a large fire pit in the center. Plants native to the Baja region were installed on the perimeter inclined bed, which was covered with red lava rocks common to Baja. The stepped down kiva-like space not only screens out views of neighboring houses, but it also immerses those in the garden. The key-hole opening in the walls provides a portal to distant mountain views and lets the garden extend out to the negative-edge drop off into the wash.

To enhance the experience of the wash and all the wildlife that are attracted to it, Martino designed a steel bridge that spans its width and connects a new desert plant garden with a sports court. This garden replaced a lawn but retains several Saguaro cacti (*Carnegiea gigantean*), which are now surrounded by other native desert plants.

Martino's use of regenerative native plants gives these gardens a push toward becoming more of a sustainable habitat. The goal was to create a livable modern garden that was undeniably desert inspired, and the clients enjoy it as much today as they did twenty years ago.

Tapered paths and low masonry walls direct movement between the auto court, studio, house, office, and guest wing.

Left: A ramp-bridge leads up to the pool pavilion through a narrow opening between masonry walls.

Left: The pavilion shades an entertaining area next to the enlarged pool deck. Martino custom designed a "floating" grill and countertop made of steel and stone that are supported on one-inch diameter steel rebar legs inspired by the client's midcentury patio furniture frames.

Above: The pavilion roof repeats the form of the house addition roof projection. It was made of industrial materials that were strong enough to cantilever six feet.

The pavilion roof is made of off-the-shelf corrugated steel attached to custom-made curved steel frames. The curves strengthen the form, and the louver configuration allows morning sun into the space and blocks the harsh afternoon sun.

Camelback Mountain dominates the view from the pavilion.

Above: Martino designed three types of safety fencing for the pool area. Aluminum flashing is woven between rebar fence posts to provide interim privacy until the front yard trees mature. Steel reinforcing bars were set in a buried concrete footing and emerge from the ground like spikes. A painted perforated metal screen wall blocks views of the driveway.

Opposite: The tilted lavender outdoor shower wall stands out like a vibrant flower against the soft gray-green tones of the desert plant palette.

A staggered, corrugated-metal fence along Canyon Walk encloses the dog run and blocks views of the neighbors.

Opposite: Steel rebar embedded in masonry mimics the whips of the native Ocotillo (*Fouquiria splendens*).

The new studio opens onto the cactus garden. The tall Saguaro cactus (*Carnegiea gigantean*) may be over 150 years old.

Curved retaining walls and a built-in concrete seat enhance the sense of enclosure around the fire pit. Steel rebar "flames" capture and radiate the heat from the fire.

From inside the garden, masonry walls function like blinders that obscure peripheral vision and focus on mountain views. The opening in the walls allows the space to flow out to the wash and connect back to the larger landscape.

Curved paths meander through the garden where hummingbirds are attracted by the right combination of plants, light, and water.

Opposite: A Gila woodpecker roosts in a Saguaro cactus (*Carnegiea gigantean*).

Paradise Valley, Arizona

CYNTHIA AND RANDY BUNESS are avid gardeners and plant collectors. Their house was built on one acre of land with much of the corner lot given up for concrete driveways and parking. An arched entry to the house itself made the interior dark. The Bunesses hired Martino to improve the appearance of the house and design places and paths as settings for their future gardening activities.

The first step was to remove as much of the concrete surface as possible and rework the driveway entrance to be more direct and take up less space. Martino replaced the arched entry with a covered terrace and added new masonry walls to form a private courtyard that is approached through an extra-wide pivot metal gate.

In the back, Martino convinced the clients to remove an existing low retaining wall behind the pool and lower the ground to the pool level making the patios and pool feel like part of the larger landscape. A simple fountain was added to recirculate the pool water and create soft sounds. On the east side of the patio are a new grill and concrete countertop attached to a masonry wall that also hides the pool equipment. Throughout the gardens, low walls provide seating and define and connect the various gardens. Martino located broad steps to further define the spaces, using them as a threshold between garden and patio.

Understanding that the Bunesses knew more about plants and gardening than he did, Martino was happy to let them take over once the garden structure was resolved and personalize the planting design. In addition to nurturing their collection of plants, they have added wonderful places to pause and rest along the paths. Martino continues to stop by to see what is new.

A custom-made steel gate and colored walls mark the entrance to the property. Beyond is the entry courtyard where walls and steps were built around existing trees.

Broad steps lead up from the pool patio to the fire pit terrace, which is bounded by a vivid blue wall.

OPEN DESERT

FIRE PLACE

GARDEN

POOL

PATIO

PATIO

RESIDENCE

AUTO COURT

ENTRY COURTYARD

0   30'

Below, opposite, and overleaf: This private botanical garden appears as lush as any deciduous forest with its variety of plants, careful composition, and path placement. Secluded seating areas are strategically interspersed.

Strong colors in horizontal
bands define the
composition of the garden.

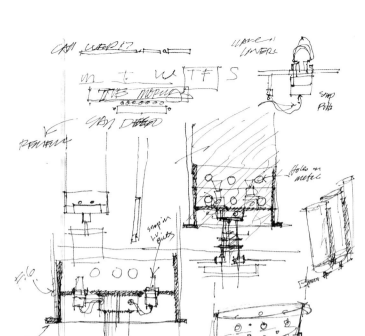

Palm Springs, California

PALMS SPRINGS GREW as a resort town in the 1950s in part because it was just within the one-hour travel time from Los Angeles that Hollywood studios allowed their actors and actresses. At that time and the following decades, George Alexander of the Alexander Construction Company and architects Dan Palmer and William Krisel built many modern houses with open floor plans and large glass walls to connect the indoor/outdoor living spaces. This garden, designed for Marc Ware, is part of a classic midcentury Alexander house, which was built on a one-third acre lot in a neighborhood where the houses are set close to the street and close to each other.

Martino recalls that he immediately understood the opportunity the site offered. He increased the usable area by about 800 square feet by moving a retaining wall to the back of the property and added a fireplace and low seat-height planters to each side of the terrace to disguise its mass. Because of a change in grade, the new nine-foot high wall is only six feet high on the uphill side where it adjoins the neighbors land.

In response to Ware's request for more entertaining space and the requirement to save three existing palm trees, Marino relocated the pool, incorporating the trees into the design. He surrounded two native California Fan Palms (*Washingtonia filifera*) with a raised planter, providing more seating and concealing unsightly air roots, and wrapped the pool around the planter. The grill was set in a concrete countertop that was poured around the trunk of the third tree.

To ensure the privacy of the master bedroom, which was compromised by the removal of a hedge, Martino installed a wall of vertical louvers that could be opened for the view and closed for privacy. The panels are custom-made translucent fiberglass shapes that are internally lit and controlled from within the house.

A bike storage shed in a "saddlebag" shape of curved fiberglass and steel panels encloses the south side and provides privacy from the adjacent neighbor. Backlighting converts the wall into a light fixture that becomes a major element of the garden.

One of Martino's favorite sayings is, "What do the neighbors have that we can use?" While he never cared for non-native Italian Cypress (*Cupressus sempervirens*), Martino saw that the neighbors on the north side had a screen of mature cypress trees next to the property line. To incorporate them in the new garden design, the trees were lit from the garden side. Palms on another adjacent property were lit in the same way, with the light fixtures installed on dimmers so that they could made to appear or disappear against the night sky.

The butterfly-shaped roof is typical of a midcentury Alexander house in Palm Springs.

Opposite: A low wall defines an entry court, where plantings and gravel have reduced the lawn area.

Martino redesigned the entry sequence with a small courtyard to connect the carport to the house and offset the entry walk from the sidewalk so that the front door is shielded from the street. A three-foot high fountain wall was added to the narrow courtyard and can be seen from the kitchen window. The front gardens originally had a large lawn and amoeba-shaped planting areas that were popular when the house was built. While Martino felt it was important for the landscape to keep the spirit of the historic midcentury modern style neighborhood, the size of the lawn was greatly reduced and free-form beds were planted with native desert plants.

This project, completed in 2005, brings midcentury design forward by half a century and offers the best sense of what is considered modern today.

Far left: A red wall terminates the view from the terrace to the south property line.

Left: The yellow fiberglass louver panels outside the master bathroom rotate for privacy or view.

Opposite: The sound of water falling from the entry fountain makes an immediate transition from the public street to the private realm.

Smooth wall and water surfaces provide the foreground and background for the seating area. Low planters flanking the space provide incidental seating. Another planter, built around the two existing Desert Fan Palm trees (*Washingtonia filifera*), projects into the pool.

Opposite: At the far end of the terrace is the dining area, where a concrete countertop wraps around an existing palm tree.

FIRE PLACE

LOW PLANTER

RAISED
PLANTER

POOL

SHED

LOUVERS

TERRACE

GRILL

COURTYARD

RESIDENCE

CARPORT

ENTRY

0   20

Left and opposite: The yellow fiberglass bike-shed panels form a backdrop for the pool and the base for mountain views. At night, the internally lit panels glow like a lantern.

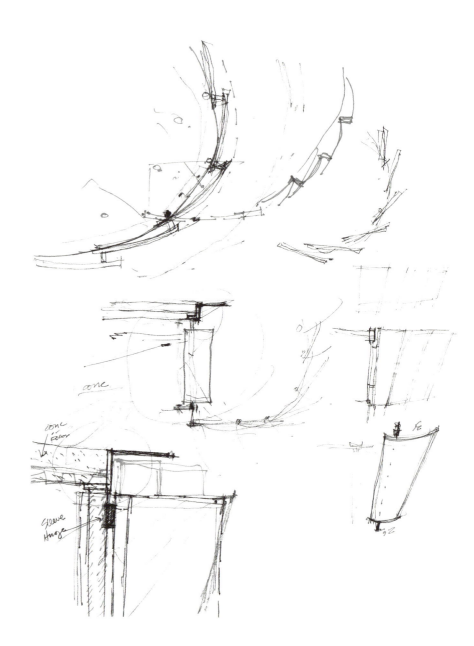

Whitewashed walls serve as the backdrop for mature Mexican Fence Post cactus (*Pachycereus marginatus*) that were relocated to this garden.

Casa Blanca Garden

Paradise Valley, Arizona

MARTINO DESIGNED OTHER GARDEN projects for Molly and Jim Larkin before they bought this nearly ninety-year-old adobe house with distinctive roof-top sleeping porches and pigeon towers. Jim Larkin, now an avid cactus lover, was introduced to the plants as a teenager when he had a job with the famed botanist Dr. Howard Gentry at the Desert Botanical Garden in Phoenix, another project that Martino had worked on.

The Larkins wanted the gardens to complement the character of the house to which they had added a new bedroom wing with an arcade that became part of a courtyard enclosure. Unusual for a project in the desert, Martino found that the two-acre property had an established garden. His job, executed over the next ten years and still on-going, was to add more cactus and trees, making gardens that now rival those of Desert Botanic Garden.

The great challenge of working on gardens with historic buildings is to design new elements that respect and even enhance what is existing and, at the same time, meet new needs. Martino used adobe-block pavers for the kitchen patio and terrace and around the pool to unite the multiple structures and traditional Ocotillo-rib fencing to enclose the courtyard. In contrast, a non-traditional lap pool and tennis court were added, and Martino used native desert plants to mediate between them and the historic buildings. The pool is adjacent and parallel to the guest wing, and its shape repeats the linear form of the building and arcade. Salvaged specimen cacti surround the pool, and the tennis court fencing was made out of cement-rubbed redwood posts and chicken wire.

This project was the first installation of Martino's now-famous prickly pear cactus roof, which started as a lark and is now eight years old. It's still doing well.

Mexican Fence post cactus (*Pachycereus marginatus*) repeat the form of the pergola posts above.

Opposite: The stone entrance driveway disrupts the land as little as possible. A similar stone path leads to the front door.

Crushed stone ground cover allows the service driveway to flow into garden paths.

Opposite: The gardens are a collection of materials and plants, some of which are very old and others are new and attest to ongoing activities.

LIBRARY
BED   BED
ARCADE
LIVING   LAP POOL
KITCHEN
PATIO
WASH
SHOP
DRIVEWAY
FIRE PLACE
TENNIS COURT
CORRAL

0   15'   30'   50'

Left: Ocotillo-rib fencing separates the kitchen patio from the gardens beyond. The wash is between the patio and the laundry building with the cacti roof.

Left bottom: Narrow paths made of adobe pavers lead to preserved old wood garden doors.

Below: For almost ten years, Prickly Pear cactus pads (*Opuntia*) on the roof have thrived and performed like any extensive green-roof plant assembly.

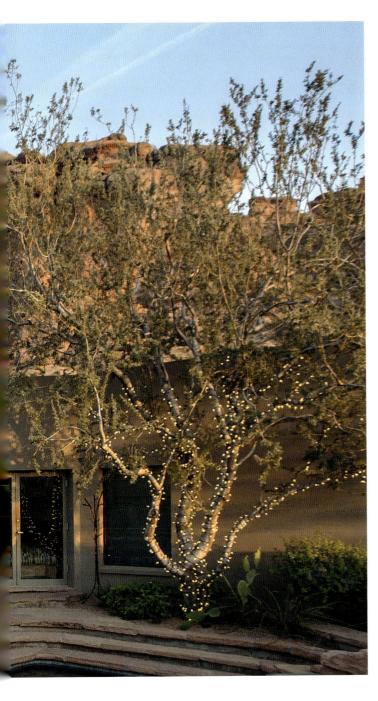

The roof of the shade is set up as an upper deck, providing additional outdoor space that is especially enjoyable at night.

Phoenix, Arizona

THE HOUSE VIRTUALLY FILLED the corner lot that Leslie and Scott Turner bought in a new development in the foothills of Camelback Mountain. There was little opportunity for garden planting, and the only hope for landscape design was to capture something of the desert beyond the property lines. Within the site, the challenge was to create new, livable outdoor space on the narrow strip of land within the 8,700 square-foot site.

The problem was unlocked by building a new garage on the existing driveway. That move addressed three issues: it freed up the existing garage to become a guest room with views of the mountain; it transformed part of the old driveway into a patio; and it created a new straight driveway with easier access from the street. The views from the new garage were so spectacular that Martino designed sliding fiberglass panels to use for two walls. These are usually kept open so the Turners can enjoy the views, but can be closed for the summer monsoons. The solid door of the old garage was replaced with sliding glass doors, which provided new views from the existing kitchen and dining room to the desert and mountains beyond the new guest room.

To improve the entry experience, Martino raised the front walls to create more privacy from the street and a sense of entrance. The new walls also created a courtyard with more welcoming spaces and better views from inside the house.

Martino enlarged a patio off the dining room that had been wedged between the house and the property line. Steps on the west side led down to the existing pool area. The original grill and counter formed the outer edge and blocked views down into the desert and wash. Martino replaced the solid handrail with wire rail panels to further open up views. The grill and counter were rebuilt against the house and the decking was expanded in its place. Thin steel columns supporting the original deck roof replaced bulky wood posts. New steel stairs lead up to a new roof deck, which doubled the entertaining space. The roof deck has a fire pit and a commanding view. Here, the garden design is found in the intimacy of small patios and courtyards, and expansive views of the desert now seen as landscape.

Higher walls transformed an exposed front yard and neighborhood overflow parking area into a small, private courtyard garden.

Opposite: The wide steel door pivots and its varied texture and color contrast with the stucco walls, concrete pavement, and desert plants. Once inside, an intimate courtyard becomes a sequence of gardens.

EXISTING POOL

ROOF DECK ABOVE

WASH

GARDEN

DINING

NEW GUEST BEDROOM
(FORMER GARAGE)

NEW PATIO

KITCHEN

ENTRY

LIVING

NEW GARAGE

MASTER
BEDROOM

OFFICE

BEDROOM

ENTRY
COURT

COURTYARD

PARKING

NEW ENTRY

0   10'

New masonry walls and yellow fiberglass doors and sliding wall panels open up the garage, which becomes an outdoor space with views toward Camelback Mountain.

DeBartolo Garden

A concrete path and steps following the contour of the hill invite ascent through the desert to the house.

Paradise Valley, Arizona

ARCHITECT JACK DEBARTOLO II and his wife, Pat, completed this contemporary two-story concrete house for their family in 1992. A key requirement was that the architecture respond to the site, which it does with an east facade of glass to take advantage of the dramatic mountain views and a solid west facade to shield the interior from the intense afternoon sun. The entire lower level is tucked into the hillside to minimize the visible volume of the building. Finally, great care was taken with the excavation to avoid damaging the land and existing vegetation beyond the building footprint.

Martino joined the team to resolve the grading issues and design the gardens. Fortunately, the house sat well on the land because the adjoining land was undisturbed and rocks excavated for the building had been removed from the property. Martino's design strategy was to develop a series of retaining walls and to manipulate the grade down the hill from the swimming pool to allow a fence-free view of the desert beyond. To this end, the pool gate and adjacent safety fence were installed below the pool rim in the time-tested English "ha-ha" landscape technique of hiding necessary barriers from one point of view in order to preserve unspoiled vistas from the other.

A series of concrete "fins" extend out from the walls and set up a rhythmic pattern, which Martino echoed in the courtyard design. According to Jack DeBartolo, "The fins hint of Palladio in evoking the arcade of a building in ruins." Martino also likes to incorporate historical references in his projects. For this garden, the nearby ruins of Frank Lloyd Wright's Rose Pauson house, which he explored as a child, provided inspiration. His memories influenced the design of the ceremonial entry steps and his response to the building fins.

The house opens onto a level turf courtyard that is strikingly different from the adjacent "wild landscape." The swimming pool was pushed up against the south retaining wall, which is tall enough to screen out views of the adjacent house. An opening in the wall just above the pool edge gives swimmers a glimpse of the valley below.

The architectural forms were so strong that Martino thought the desert garden just needed to be itself, spare and rugged. After the walls were built, mature desert trees were planted in key places, and other new plants were installed small or even planted as seeds. The idea was that the landscape would be allowed to grow over time. New native Blue Palo Verde (*Parkinsonia florida*) and Desert Ironwood (*Olneya tesota*) trees provide the backbone of the garden, and common Creosote bush (*Larrea tridentate*) and Brittlebush (*Encelia farinose*) join the surrounding untouched desert plant community.

With this landscape approach, this contemporary concrete, steel, and glass house sits well in its desert location.

Opposite: Unadorned concrete walls make a distinct backdrop for a rugged desert garden.

Opposite bottom and below: The concrete "fin" walls were designed for the garden to correspond to the building "fins." From the other direction, they bracket views from the courtyard toward Camelback Mountain.

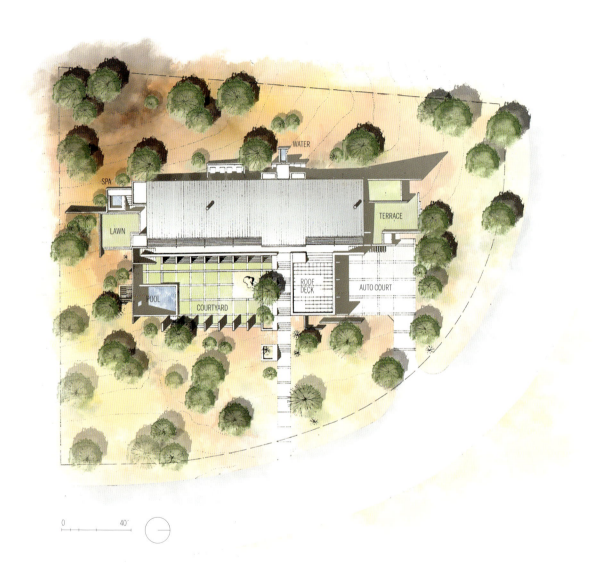

SPA

LAWN

WATER

TERRACE

POOL

COURTYARD

ROOF DECK

AUTO COURT

0   40'

Opposite top: The entry stair continues up to the second-level entry and roof deck above the garage, which is a primary outdoor living space with a 180-degree view of the surrounding mountains.

Opposite bottom: Alternating streams of light and cast shadows reinforce the effect of the fin pattern and dynamically mediate between the regular built geometry and the variety of desert plant forms.

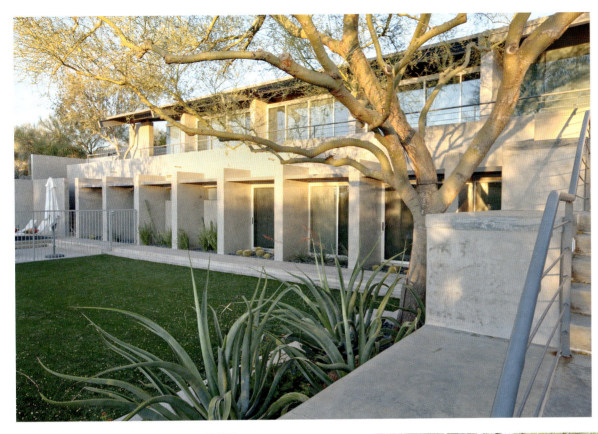

The shape of the pool complements the house and garden wall forms. A window in the far wall at water level allows a view to the south. The pool surface reflects the sky and the wall surface captures the tree shadows further connecting the garden to the site. The safety gate is below the courtyard so that the view of the desert is uninterrupted from the pool and terrace.

Groups of desert plants are clustered beneath a Prosopis thornless hybrid 'AZT' Mesquite tree, which was propagated by the client.

Mesa, Arizona

THE ONLY MAN-MADE MARK on this nearly pristine five-acre desert site was an old jeep trail that led to a clearing. Martino worked closely with architect John Douglas, the client's son, to site the house on the property to maximize mountain views and preserve as much of the virgin desert as possible. The clearing became the place for the house and the drive followed the trail.

On the site the clients, Marilyn and Cliff Douglas, found abundant wildlife in the surrounding washes that the animals use as corridors. The entry path was made six feet wide to give rattlesnakes a wide berth. The patio walls are railing height from the pool side, but at least five feet high from the outside, providing both protection from predators and the required pool safety enclosure. Hose bib handles have to be removable because the javalina (peccary) learn how to turn the water on to make muddy wallows. Lesser nighthawks swoop in and drink from the swimming pool on the fly. On one site visit, Martino rescued a rare Sonoran Gila monster (a venomous lizard) from the pool and discovered that they have a frightening hiss when angry.

Unlike most Martino projects, this landscape design lent itself to curved forms. The driveway had to curve around mature trees and avoid large Saguaro cacti (*Carnegiea gigantean*), which are protected by local codes. The paths also follow the topography with small bridges across washes. Martino repeated the curved shape for the entry wall leading to the house. Disturbed areas next to the house were restored with native plants and new trees were planted along the driveway. Native wildflower seeds were spread near the house.

This project brought Cliff Douglas and Martino together, and they formed an association to grow desert trees in a nursery called Arid Zone Trees. This nursery made desert trees commercially available for the first time on a large scale in the country. Martino's work on this project received a state ASLA award in 1988 and it was his first project to receive a national ASLA award for environmental excellence that same year. The Douglas Garden continues to showcase plants that combine the hardy traits needed to survive in these conditions with the desired characteristics for a garden in the desert.

Left: All changes to the site work around these spectacular large Saguaro cacti (*Carnegiea gigantean*).

Below: A low curved masonry wall guides movement from the driveway to the entry. In the garden retaining walls and low steps divide planted spaces and paths.

Shady clearings offer places
to sit and watch the wildlife.

Patios with low walls are
transitional spaces between
the house and desert gardens.

TENNIS COURT

DESERT

CARPORT

WASH

WILDFLOWERS & WEEDS

DESERT

DRIVE

RESIDENCE

FOUNTAIN

WASH

ENTRY

POOL

ENTRY WALLS

WILDFLOWERS & WEEDS

WILDFLOWERS & WEEDS

DESERT

GUEST HOUSE

WASH

0   40'

A profusion of desert plants growing in planters and containers animates the pool deck and terrace. The wall around the pool is higher on the desert side to protect the house from wildlife.

Scottsdale, Arizona

Decorative openings in the masonry walls allow the breeze into the courtyard, but there is still privacy and a sense of enclosure. The blocks are no longer manufactured, but Martino came up with a suitable match.

MUCH OF THE PHOENIX/SCOTTSDALE AREA was developed in the 1960s. The Schreiber Brothers designed many modernist houses, which are highly sought after today. After purchasing their house, Jennifer and Richard Linder went on an tour of midcentury houses in Palm Springs to look for ideas and discovered Martino's work.

The Linder house was a typical midcentury house, with a front facade with a large expanse of glass and no privacy from the street. The entry walk was combined with the driveway, and the perimeter walls were too low to screen the neighboring houses. Like many of Martino's clients, the Linders wanted gardens that were integrated into the house design to create outdoor rooms.

Martino took advantage of a little-used zoning opportunity that allowed for a portion of the front yard to be enclosed by a six-foot-high wall. This space became a new entry courtyard with a path from the street that was separate from the driveway. The courtyard wall completely blocks out street views and makes a new outdoor room. Native plants have replaced the bare ground, turning it into a "wild" desert garden.

In the rear, Martino replaced a section of the low wall along the alley with a new eight-foot-high masonry wall, which became the focus of the view from the house. To block views from the house to the west, Martino designed "shoji screens" made of corrugated metal and cement board panels to make thin privacy panels. These were built in sections and staggered to create interest and shadows. The existing pool was retained, and new concrete pavement was added to connect it to the house. In a typical Martino design move, part of the deck was removed to allow planting to go to the water's edge.

The flow of space through the open plan and the integration of interior and exterior characteristic of modern design are now enhanced by gardens framed by walls that define distinct spaces and encourage more living outdoors.

In front of the house, dense
plantings add color and
habitat to the streetscape.

An entry walk and courtyard wall were built around a large Saguaro cactus (*Carnegiea gigantean*) that anchors the planting design in the front yard garden. The new courtyard connects directly to the interior of the house through sliding glass doors.

ALLEY

POOL

PATIO

LAWN

BEDROOM

KITCHEN

GUEST HOUSE

BEDROOM

RESIDENCE

CARPORT

COURTYARD

DRIVEWAY

STREET

0   20'

The thin "shoji" screen walls were a relatively inexpensive way to block views of the adjacent house.

Opposite: Tall plantings in the corner of the red wall screen views of the alley and neighboring houses. On the opposite side of the pool, a yellow wall defines one edge of the patio.

Below: Downlighting animates the wall and the water at night.

Kotoske Garden

A wall opening showcases an existing Organ Pipe cactus (*Stenocereus thurberi*).

Paradise Valley, Arizona

ANDREA AND TOM KOTOSKE WERE NEWLY arrived in Phoenix when they discovered Martino's gardens with colored walls. He initially declined their request that he design one for them, but he quickly reconsidered when they mentioned that their house had been designed by Blaine Drake, one of Frank Lloyd Wright's original apprentices at Taliesin. In 1945 Drake started his own practice in Arizona, and Martino had been studying his work since the 1960s.

At the Kotoske house, a previous owner had covered the original stacked block walls with stucco and added a freestanding garage. Fortunately, the house was otherwise unaltered. The clients intended to expand the interior space by enclosing the long drive-thru carport, and they had already removed its roof. Their next step was to cut off the distinctive roof overhangs and replace them with parapet walls. Horrified, Martino told them to stop. On his second visit, he shared his file of Drake's architecture and sketched how he thought Drake might have handled the west facade and new entry. Based on the sketches, the Kotoskes asked Martino to redesign their house and nearly one-and-one-half acre garden. Their plan was to turn the carport into a family room, laundry, and guest bedroom since there already was a separate garage.

This was a dream assignment because the design could determine how interior and exterior spaces related to each other. Martino devised a method of economically adding sliding glass pocket doors to existing walls. In total, four sets of these disappearing walls were used, including a set at each end of the new family room. The asphalt driveway was replaced with crushed rock and realigned to enhance the arrival experience. New courtyards were added at either end of the long family room. When the glass walls are opened, the family room and courtyards combine into a single 90-foot-long entertaining space with fountains in both courtyards that bookend the garden.

Other small courtyards and gardens surround the house. Some gardens are intimate and contained while others are open to mountain views. Existing trees and hedges that blocked these views were removed. Martino replaced non-native trees and shrubs with dozens of desert native plants, some of which were relocated from other areas on the site. He also took cuttings from existing plants for subsequent garden projects.

The garden was completed in 2000, but the clients still call Martino back for more small projects. The changes, especially to the gardens and the ability of the house to open up to them, took this project into the next century. Martino's new design preserved the work of Blaine Drake and at the same time created a home that graciously serves a contemporary lifestyle.

COURTYARD

GARAGE

PARKING

BED

BED

BED

ENTRY
COURTYARD

PATIO

LIVING

BASKETBALL
COURT

POOL

FAMILY
ROOM

GUEST

SPA

PATIO

DRIVEWAY

0   10'   25'

Rusted steel panels are juxtaposed with a deep purple wall, a contrast of both color and texture.

The tall masonry wall screens views of the neighbor's house while the sound of splashing water drowns out the noise from a nearby highway.

Lantana plants grow like vines and cover the metal shade screen. The flowers attract butterflies and hummingbirds to the garden.

Opposite: The quiet pool sits beside the entry gates at one cnd of thc ncw family room assembly of indoor/outdoor spaces.

A poolside fountain wall was strategically positioned to block unwanted views. Recirculated water splashes onto the pool deck and then flows into the pool. The flush edge spa spills into a lower pool of water and adds more sounds to the garden.

Opposite: The basketball court fence was made of welded wire mesh, which is usually used to reinforce concrete slabs. The Blue Palo Verde (*Parkinsonia florida*) trees cast golden light when in bloom.

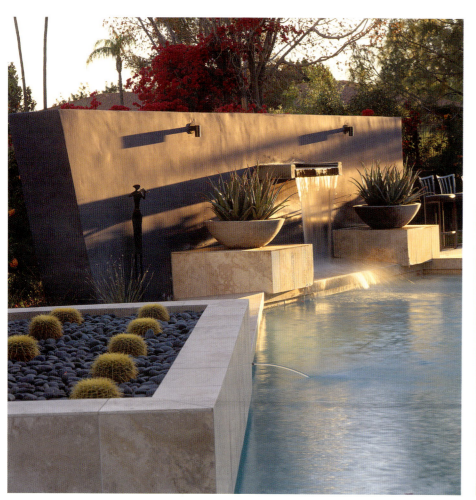

A spectacular site with distinctive boulders and sweeping views of the desert valley asks for a landscape design that is uncluttered and sparse.

Goldman Garden

Scottsdale, Arizona

THIS HOUSE SITS ON A STEEP HILLSIDE surrounded by desert landscape made up of hundreds of house-sized boulders and large Saguaro cactus (*Carnegiea gigantean*). Lisa and Bruce Goldman bought it in 2012 even though its faux-Tuscan style and curved garden forms did not suit their modernist taste. To remedy that situation, they commissioned Martino to adapt the style of the house to something more contemporary, make strong connections to the seventeen-acre desert site, and maximize the spectacular views. The initial work required removing distracting elements such as the boulder-lined "lagoon-style" pool and and its heavy wrought-iron railings.

Martino's new pool and terrace design has simple and elegant forms. The lap part of the pool extends out toward the rocky mountainside. A glass railing allows it to look as if it is part of the desert. To reduce the need for new retaining walls, the new rectangular pool was built on pylons within the existing curved retaining walls, which are now hidden below the water surface. A fountain wall in Martino's signature red blocks the downhill view into the neighboring property.

Many curved exterior house walls were modified with floor-to-ceiling glass pocket doors. When they are open, the travertine floor runs continuously from the entry through the living room and terrace to the edge of the water. The terrace functions as an observation deck, overlooking the spectacular landscape.

Martino designed a small terrace at the entry that is just large enough for two chairs and a table. From there, the uphill view is as spectacular as the valley view on the opposite side of the house. The final design touch was a shallow water trough that has become a "neighborhood watering hole" attracting birds and wildlife.

Opposite and below: A colorful low wall is a welcoming marker between the auto court and the path to the entry terrace.

Right: Another red wall marks the edge of the pool behind the house.

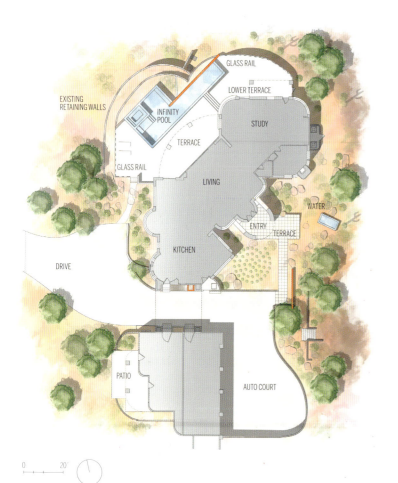

EXISTING
RETAINING WALLS

GLASS RAIL

INFINITY
POOL

TERRACE

GLASS RAIL

LIVING

DRIVE

KITCHEN

PATIO

AUTO COURT

GLASS RAIL

LOWER TERRACE

STUDY

WATER

ENTRY
TERRACE

0   20'

The brilliant red pool
wall is a foil for views of the
rocky landscape beyond.

The uphill view from the entry garden is filled with non-native cacti and a small four-inch-deep concrete water trough that attracts wildlife and allows them to walk in from the uphill side.

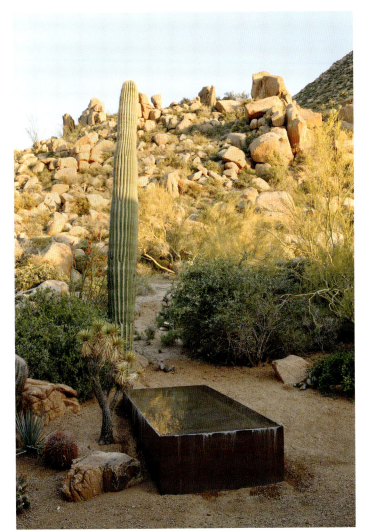

This design is a composition of shapes and colors that focus, layer, and direct views. The deep-red fiberglass counter glows at night and becomes a garden light fixture.

Palm Springs, California

LAS PALMAS IS THE SECOND GARDEN Martino designed for Marc Ware in Palm Springs. In 2005, after he sold Dry Falls, Ware hired architect Don Boss of Sun Valley, Idaho, to design a new house and Martino to design the gardens, with the unusual charge to make them "groovy, cool, and sexy."

The majority of Martino's residential projects are renovations so the opportunity to be on a design team from the start was particularly welcome. On this project, he designed all the site work from scratch. One of his major goals was to create a seamless indoor-outdoor experience where all doors led to patios. Ware wanted intimate garden areas for entertaining and solitude as well as an open, level lawn and tennis court that could also be used for occasional large gatherings and fund-raising events. Martino positioned the primary constructed garden elements — pools, fire pit, fiberglass follies — as focal points. They define space, guide circulation, and create long views through the gardens.

Martino wanted this design to relate to the rugged canyons of the adjacent San Jacinto Mountains and to be an example of a low-water consuming plant palette of cacti and succulents. Martino hoped the theatrical design would create a buzz and generate interest in using desert plants. Life-sustaining water savings would naturally follow. Ordinary desert plants were showcased by creating scenes to draw attention to their dramatic form. As a result, the choices of materials, details, and appropriate desert plants turn toward the future without ignoring the unmistakable character of Palm Springs.

The theme of the garden is the celebration of water and light. The first is typically scarce and precious in the desert, and the second abundant. The swimming pool and ten additional water pools all have infinity or flush edges and function as reflecting pools. Tall masonry walls were placed to create shade and catch shadows. Frosted glass walls block views and create screens to collect interesting shadows during the day and at night because of the back lighting. The translucent fiberglass elements glow when back-lit by sunlight during the day and become light fixtures at night. The folly-like outdoor shower and its twin, the outdoor urinal, act as objects of interest in the garden.

Illuminated gates beckon guests in the evening. By day, the frosted glass and reflecting pool make a transition from the street.

Houses in this exclusive neighborhood are usually hidden behind tall hedges with entries through an inconspicuous gate. Here Martino set the entrance gates forty-four feet back from the curb and created an entry garden that hints at the landscape beyond. This garden is noticeably different from the adjacent clipped hedges and Mediterranean-type planting of the area. There were ninety-two California Fan Palm trees (*Washingtonia filifera*) on the property when Martino started his design, some of which are sixty-five feet tall. All were retained either where found and Martino designed around them, or were relocated. Shorter palms were used for the planter islands in the pool. Dense plantings were added to the perimeter where the five-foot height limit for a fence was too low to provide privacy, especially since the floor level was five feet above the street beyond the pool.

This project has become the quintessential midcentury desert modern garden, even if it took a half century and a designer from Arizona to find its full expression.

Left: The monumental wall beyond the auto court frames a view of existing California Fan palm trees (*Washingtonia filifera*).

Below: The syncopated ocher-colored Domino Wall in a side cactus garden is made of corbelled cinder blocks with a smooth stucco finish.

Opposite: A sculpture by Los Angeles artist Robert Toll sits on a fiberglass bench that glows at night in the cactus sculpture garden that includes Whale's Tongue agave (*Agave olatifolia*), Golden Barrel cactus (*Echinocactus grusonii*), Silver Torch cactus (*Cleistocactus strausii*), Mexican Fence Post cactus (*Pachycereus marginatus*), and Ocotillo (*Fouquiria splendens*).

From the entry bridge, the view through the house to the pool is unobstructed. The interior floor, pool deck, and water are on the same level, giving a continuous sense of space.

Tall California Fan Palm trees (*Washingtonia filifera*) are ubiquitous in Palm Springs, an oasis in the desert surrounded by rugged mountains. The garden's palm trees provide continuity with the hundreds of palms trees beyond the property.

In front of the Casita, a long pool separates the patios. Planter islands with Cereus cactus (*Cereus peruvianus*) provide sculptural definition.

Far left: Illuminated yellow fiberglass roof panels shade the Ramada.

Left and below: A water runnel goes through the cactus garden and connects the fire pit area and the Ramada, which has a limestone table with a slot that is used to cool wine bottles. Martino found inspiration for this detail from the Cardinal's Garden at Villa Lante.

Opposite: The fire pit has three curved concrete benches and terminates the long axis that starts in the living room and front yard cactus sculpture garden.

Below: Water tables and island planters are interspersed with shaded seating areas.

Opposite: The angled walls of the green fiberglass outdoor shower complement the red fireplace wall.

Phoenix, Arizona

A small tabletop landscape composed of a Golden Barrel Cactus (*Echinocactus grusonii*), a pot of rocks, and a concrete house made by Larry Kornegay, a frequent collaborator of Martino's.

JANE AND STEVE MARTINO HAVE LIVED in this suburban Phoenix house for nearly fifteen years, raising their two sons and caring for more dogs and cats than they can count. The gardens surrounding the house and office studio include all the familiar Martino design elements that shield his private gardens from unwanted views to and from adjoining houses, streets, and an alley.

The original driveway was turned into an entry courtyard that is enclosed by a six-foot-high red masonry wall. Lengthy maneuvering with the building inspectors over which side of this corner lot is the legal front allowed this height, which is otherwise limited to three feet. Thus made into a private space, the entry courtyard has a recessed fireplace with an extended raised hearth aligned with the new living room to better connect the spaces. Mature shade trees keep the south side of the house cool.

There is a small bosque of Palo Verde trees (*Parkinsonia x Desert Museum*) in the Court of the Felines. Martino tried this hybrid here because it blooms prolifically, although this turned out to be a maintenance nuisance. On the east side of the courtyard, Martino planted cacti on the storage shed roof, which is his version of a "green" roof.

When Martino moved his office to a home studio, Jane asked if he could replicate the curved bench in his office courtyard in their backyard. As often happens with Martino's projects, the backyard was turned into a courtyard with several enclosing walls. Here Martino experiments with wall colors to see how they look in the bright sunlight or dappled shade. He also experiments with plants that grow in containers so he can move them to different exposures and try out various compositions of plant palettes. Friends who operate nurseries exchange cuttings with Martino in an effort to better understand their habits. Eventually, these plants are likely to become part of another Martino-designed garden. Martino welds custom-designed metal garden elements in an outdoor shop, which has walls to block the noise and not bother the neighbors.

This is a garden that takes time to absorb because its design reflects the dynamic nature of the plants and the landscape architect, who are both constantly evolving. And like other Martino gardens, even if it doesn't shout, "I'm different, just to be different," visitors certainly are aware that it is a special place.

Opposite: Tall red walls conceal the private garden beyond.

Right: A Blue Palo Verde tree (*Parkinsonia florida*) against a red wall is a reoccurring pairing in Martino gardens.

Left: The fireplace in the entry courtyard encourages outdoor living on cool winter evenings.

Right: Martino experiments with plant communities throughout the garden to see how they respond and support each other including a Staghorn Cholla (*Opuntia versicolor*).

Overleaf left: In the Court of the Felines, four Palo Verde trees (*Parkinsonia x Desert Museum*) carpet the ground with golden blossoms.

Overleaf right: The cactus shed has a Prickly Pear cactus (*Opuntia*) garden on the roof.

ALLEY   SHED

OUTDOOR SHOP

SHOP

PATIO

PORCH

OFFICE

WEEDS & WILDFLOWERS

COURT OF THE FELINES

CACTUS ROOF SHED

EXISTING RESIDENCE

ENTRY COURTYARD

CARPORT

0   20'

Left: The former grass backyard was transformed into a self-contained courtyard by an eight-foot-high shed wall that screens views of the houses across the alley. The curved site-cast concrete bench provides a unifying element to the ever-changing collection of plants.

Opposite: A Stickman cactus (*Nopalea cochenillifera*) is thriving in this ideal location.

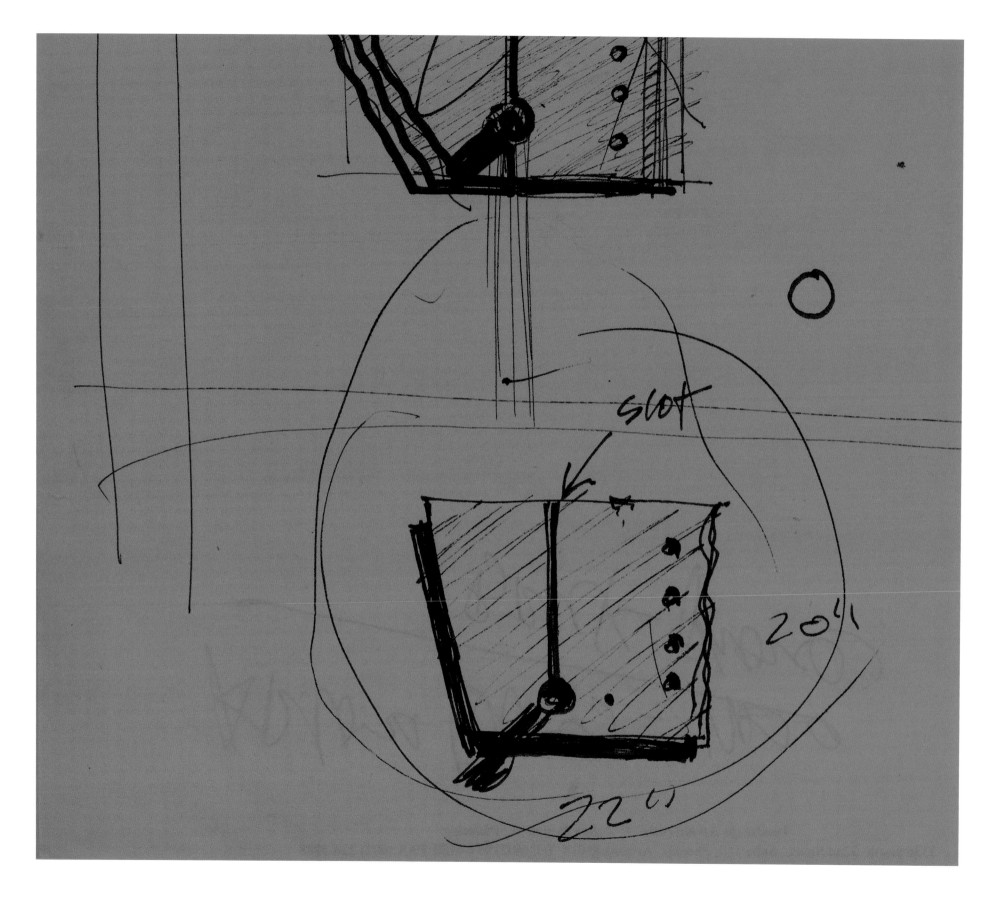

slot

20"

22"

I would like to thank my wife, Jane, for her patience as I worked hundreds of late nights trying to run my practice and perfect my designs.

Without clients I would never have had a practice, and I'd like to especially thank the early pioneer clients who appreciated the desert and let me install "weeds" in their projects (without a fight) as well as the numerous clients who taught me much about design and horticulture.

I owe thanks to the consultants and contractors that helped make my projects what they are and to the scores of employees over the decades that have helped me. I'd like to thank my associate, Gosia Okolowicz, for the wonderful site plans in the book and her support team of Tyler Forgacs, Lora Martens, Alba Rodriguez, Idaly Corella, and Roman Cervantes.

I want to acknowledge my friend and fellow procrastinator Steve Gunther who has been photographing my projects for twenty years with the idea of someday doing a book.

This book would not have happened without the writing, energy, and diligence of Caren Yglesias, who not only knew the publishing world, but had to double as a drill sergeant to make the two Steves stay focused.

—S.M.

I thank Steve Martino for his commitment to publish his designs of desert gardens and his confidence in my ability to "quarterback" this book. We are all grateful for the expert guidance of Elizabeth White at The Monacelli Press, and the design skill of David Blankenship. Together they turned a collection of garden pictures and words into a monograph of Martino's extraordinary work.

I also thank Terry Clements, program chair of Virginia Tech's landscape architecture program, for bringing me, an architect, into the world of landscape architecture with her dedication to students and clear vision of the profession's responsibilities and opportunities that sets such a good example for us all. And, with unbounded love, I appreciate the support of my husband, John Livengood.

—C.Y.

I would like to express my deep appreciation to Joanne Jaffe, editor of *Angeles Magazine,* for suggesting I try my hand at garden photography and ultimately making me the magazine's garden photographer. I'm grateful to *Sunset* magazine for introducing me to Steve Martino and his work. Thank you very much, Steve Martino, for creating awesome gardens for me to photograph.

—S.G.

First published in the United States by The Monacelli Press.

Library of Congress Control Number 2107962354
ISBN 978 158093 491-9

Design by David Blankenship for Because

Text set in Bcnton Sans

Printed in China

The Monacelli Press
6 West 18th Street
New York, New York 10011

www.monacellipress.com